SPANISH FLAVORS

JOSÉ PIZARRO'S
SPANISH FLAVORS

PHOTOGRAPHY BY EMMA LEE

KYLE BOOKS

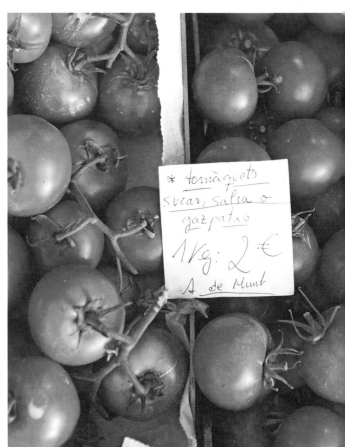

* tomàquets
sucar, salsa o
gazpatxo
1 Kg: 2 €
A de Munt

Published in 2012 by Kyle Books
an imprint of Kyle Cathie Limited
www.kylebooks.com

Distributed by National Book Network
4501 Forbes Blvd., Suite 200
Lanham, MD 20706
Phone: (800) 462-6420
Fax: (301) 429-5746
custserv@nbnbooks.com

ISBN: 978-1-906868-89-5

10 9 8 7 6 5 4 3 2 1

Editor: Sophie Allen
Designer: Peter Dawson, www.gradedesign.com
Designer's assistant: Louise Evans
Photographer: Emma Lee
Photographer's assistant: Rahel Weiss
Props stylist: Lesley Dilcock
Food stylist: Debbie Major
Copy editor: Stephanie Evans
Americanizer: Lee Faber
Production: Gemma John and Nic Jones

Library of Congress Control Number is available online.

Printed in China by 1010 Printing International Ltd.

CONTENTS

INTRODUCTION

I was sitting in a bar in the port of San Sebastian in October 2010 during one of my many trips to Spain, looking for new ingredients and dishes for my new restaurants. I was enjoying a glass of txacoli, the local zesty dry white wine, while thinking about the theme for my new book. I was churning over ideas about what it should be about: ingredients, the regions, the history, the producers, and how I could bring all this together. I was getting more and more confused because there are just so many things to say about Spain. I think that Spain is like seventeen different countries all rolled into one. With the second glass of txacoli, things started to become clearer. It seemed logical to me that the regions of Spain, with their unique historical and climatic influences, and their best-known ingredients, should form the basis of the book.

Spain is a very large country, and so it seemed simplest just to divide it into the north, the east, the center, the south, and the islands.

The North—Galicia, Asturias, Cantabria, Basque Country, Rioja, and **Navarra** —once one of the poorest regions, albeit very rich in gastronomic delights, is surrounded on two sides by the colder waters of the North Atlantic ocean, and on the other, by the Cantabria sea. It has the greatest rainfall in Spain, and is a mixture of mountains and green pastures, which influences not only the local ingredients, but also the type of cuisine; seafood plays a great part, as does milk, and therefore cheese, pork is invariably salted, the vegetables are robust, such as cabbage, potatoes, and dried beans, and there are chestnuts and cider from the abundant apple trees. As a result, the dishes are warming and filling, yet inexpensive to produce, and also highlight the two main occupations of the region, fishing and farming.

The East—Catalonia, Valencia, and **Murcia**—runs along the Mediterranean shoreline, where the food appears to be almost more European and Mediterranean than Iberian. The ingredients here are influenced by the land and the sea: wild mushrooms and game from the mountains that border with France, vegetables from the fertile Ebro delta, fish and shellfish from the rocky shoreline, rice from the Albufera, and citrus fruits from the warm fertile plains of the south.

The Center—Aragón, Castilla y León, Extremadura, Madrid, and **Castilla La Mancha**, is made up of the only landlocked regions of Spain, which are more arid and flat, with extremes of temperature between the summer and winter. Here there can be nine months of hell and "a three-month freeze," as the locals put it. History plays an especially big part in the food of this region. The *conquistadores* who left Spain and discovered the new world brought back with them not only gold and silver, but also potatoes, corn, tomatoes, pumpkins, and red peppers from which the famous Spanish *pimentón* is made. The cork oak forests of the southern areas provide the perfect grazing for the Ibérico pig from which fresh pork and the more famous air-dried hams of Spain are produced, as well as chorizo, the traditional pork sausage flavored with garlic and *pimentón*. Lentils and chickpeas are popular here and the saffron from the flat plains of La Mancha is considered to be the best in the world, along with Spain's most famous cheese, Manchego.

The South—Andalucia—is greatly influenced not only by its proximity to two seas, the Atlantic Ocean and the Mediterranean, but also the invasion of the Moors who ruled the region for over 800 years. They introduced a system of irrigation which helped to water what was previously a very dry area; they brought with them sun-loving fruits such as citrus fruits, strawberries, peaches, cherries, quince, and dates, and vegetables such as eggplant and spinach; they introduced spices from the east into the local cuisine, and the tradition of sweet pastries and desserts. The coastline produces some of the best seafood in Spain: prawns, cuttlefish, and anchovies from Huelva, and tuna from Cadiz, octopus, sardines, red bream, and red mullet. The food of this region goes with the climate, including as it does fresh (often chilled) dishes such as gazpacho and salads; and it was again the Moors who introduced the way of eating a collection of small dishes, known as mezze in the Middle East, which became tapas in my home country of Spain.

The islands—the Balearics of **Majorca**, **Minorca**, and **Ibiza** to the east of the mainland, and the volcanic Canary Islands of **La Palma**, **La Gomera**, **El Hierro**, **Gran Canaria**, **Ternerife**, **Fuerteventura**, and **Lanzarote** far from the south of Spain, sitting in the South Atlantic, off the coast of the African Sahara desert—have developed their own styles of cooking, based largely around the crops they grow, the influences of nearby countries, and again, the human history. Although the islands of Spain are very different from each other, it seemed logical to group them together as "the islands," because, being separated from the mainland, they are wonderfully distinct.

When you go through the book, you will see ingredients that you might think are situated in the wrong area. The reason they are in a particular section is because they are linked to my memories of traveling around Spain. This is not just about Spanish cuisine, but about Spanish ingredients and my interpretation. I'm so lucky to be living in London, and to be inspired by all the different cuisines that this city has.

THE NORTH

THE NORTH: INTRODUCTION

Northern Spain is famous for its gastronomy throughout the world. This vast land, bounded by mountains and seas, is rich in culinary resources and has a generations-old tradition of excellent food and drink. These mountains produce cheese, dairy, and pork products that vie with the very finest of any country. And I think the beef from the north is the best in Spain. Thriving fishing communities dot the long coastlines, landing fish and seafood of superlative quality on countless quaysides. Within this northern area, protected from external influence by its terrain, are distinct regions rightly proud of their profoundly separate identities and personalities, differences that are reinforced in the Basque Country and Galicia by maintaining their own languages.

When people ask me which part of Spain is my favorite, in food terms, I have to say the north. To me, culinary heaven would be to start eating in the Basque Country and to tour the entire north, ending in Galicia. San Sebastián has more Michelin-starred restaurants than anywhere in the world and I try to visit twice a year to experience as many of them as I can, but my favorite remains Arzak, both for its food and the brilliant foodie conversations I have with my friends Elena and her father Juan Mari Arzak. San Sebastián is so much more than Michelin stars and the New Basque Cuisine—it is also about the pintxos bars and their simple, yet utterly delicious dishes that celebrate local seasonal ingredients.

Rioja, renowned for its wonderful wines, has also become a destination for culture tourists as well as gourmets. Beautiful boutique hotels, modern art and architecture sit happily with the centuries-old vineyards and bodegas. Lovers of good food must also try the chorizo from this region and, of course, cook it in Rioja wine. And the cauliflower from Calahorra is the most sublime cauliflower you will ever try.

Navarra, one of the country's "market gardens," produces outstanding artichokes, peas, fava beans, and white asparagus, which we Spanish love. Don't be surprised to read on some jars of asparagus the word "cojonudos," which literally means "big balls." This is a reference to a visit by King Carlos to a factory where he tried the white asparagus and proclaimed "Cojonudos!" meaning really delicious! The best way to eat asparagus is simply steamed or roasted with some very good mayonnaise or just olive oil and Ibérico ham. Navarra's other famous ingredient is the piquillo pepper, small, pointed, and slightly piquant, which is used to flavor the lamb chilindróns (stews) of this region.

I remember Cantabria from childhood holidays with my family. One of my lasting memories is the first time I experienced that sweet smell of anchovies. Vast quantities of tuna, sardines, and anchovies from the Bay of Biscay are prepared in the many family-owned seafood restaurants along the coast. Cantabria is also well known for its dairy products— quesada pasiega, a type of cheesecake, is a speciality of this region.

I go to Asturias as often as I can. This is where my friend Nacho Manzano has a great restaurant, Casa Marcial—you must order *arroz con pitu de caleya* (rice with free-range chicken), and of course the region's signature dish—*fabada asturiana* (a pot of slow-cooked white beans, shoulder of pork or lacón gallego, chorizo, morcilla, and often saffron). And don't forget to drink it with the local cider!

We end this culinary odyssey in Galicia, like the pilgrims who reach Santiago de Compostella. Galicia is famous for its fish and seafood from the Atlantic, including scallops, whose shell, the symbol of St. James the Apostle, has been carried by pilgrims since the Middle Ages. The best-known white wine here is Albariño, but promise me you will try the Godello and finish your meal with a shot of *orujo*, a local digestif.

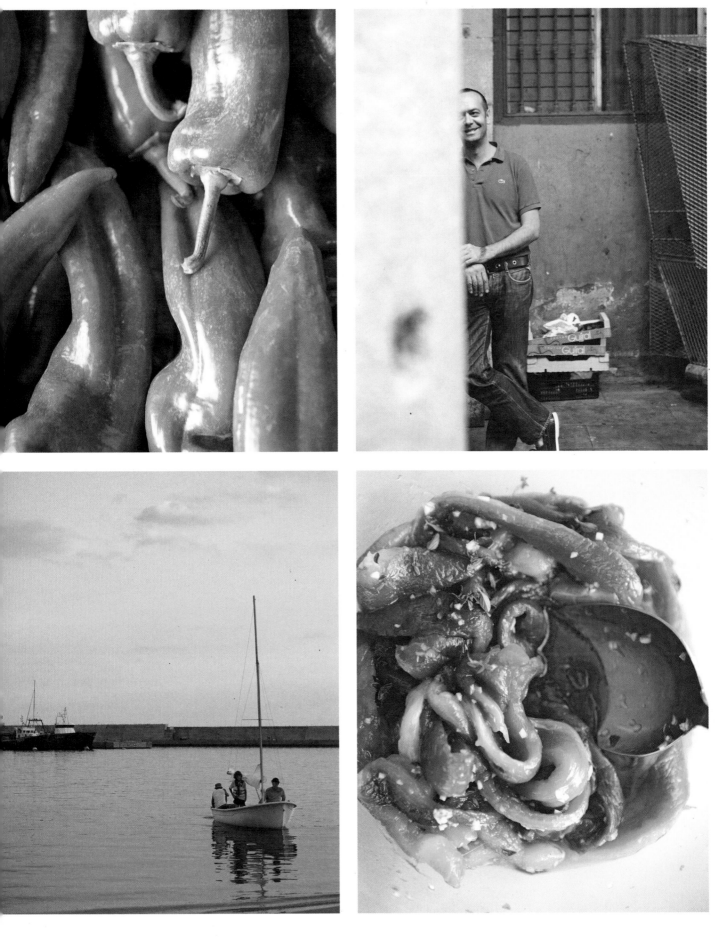

Artichoke, asparagus, and fennel salad with crab

The best globe artichokes traditionally come from Navarra, the market garden of Spain, thanks to the fertile plains flanking the Ebro River. However, many people all over Spain now grow artichokes in their own gardens, and I particularly enjoy those from my father's garden in Talaván in Extremadura. His favorite way of eating them is either boiled, then cut into wedges and sautéed in olive oil, or simmered in a salt cod and potato stew. In this recipe, the fresh flavors from the green vegetables combine well with the sweetness of the crab. The white asparagus from this area is hugely popular in Spain—the only way I like to eat them is with mayonnaise.

Serves 4

4 large globe artichokes	
juice of 1 lemon, plus 1 tablespoon	
8 oz bunch of fine asparagus spears	
6 oz fennel bulb	
½ teaspoon Dijon mustard	
3 tablespoons extra-virgin olive oil	
8 oz fresh white crabmeat	
2 tablespoons olive oil mayonnaise (see page 227)	
1 tablespoon chopped herb fennel or flat-leaf parsley	
sea salt and freshly ground black pepper	

Working with one artichoke at a time, cut off the stalk and the dark green leaves from the base of the globe. Then cut off the top half with a large sharp knife and break away the remaining leaves until you reach the hairy choke at the center. Slice the choke off the base with a small sharp knife, and drop the base into a bowl of water acidulated with the juice of 1 lemon. Repeat with the rest of the artichokes.

Break off and discard the woody ends from each asparagus spear, and cut the rest of the stalks into 2-inch pieces. Drop them into a pan of boiling salted water, and cook for 2 minutes until tender. Remove with a slotted spoon to a colander, refresh under cold water, then drain well on paper towels. Add the artichoke bases to the boiling water, bring back to a boil, and cook for 6–7 minutes or until just tender. Drain, refresh with cold water, and leave to drain well on paper towels.

Thinly shave the fennel bulb, on a mandoline or by hand, put into a bowl of ice water and leave for 5 minutes to crisp up. Meanwhile, whisk the remaining tablespoon of lemon juice with the Dijon mustard, then gradually whisk in the olive oil, and some salt and pepper to taste. Drain the fennel and dry well (a salad spinner is ideal for this). Slice the artichoke bases crosswise into thin slices, and toss in a bowl with the asparagus, shaved fennel, and lemon vinaigrette.

Put the crabmeat into a bowl and gently stir in the mayonnaise, chopped herb fennel or parsley, and seasoning to taste. Spoon some of the artichoke salad and crab salad onto each plate. Drizzle the remaining dressing from the artichokes over the top and around the outside of the plate, and serve.

Sautéed artichokes with cockles and jamón

The first time I encountered this dish was in La Taverna del Clinic in Barcelona with my friend Enric. I was instantly smitten by the earthy flavor imparted to the dish by the artichokes, and the saltiness of the cockles. This is my version of that dish. The best cockles I've ever eaten were in the north of Spain, which is why I have put this recipe in the North chapter.

Serves 4

12 young globe artichokes

juice of 1½ large lemons, plus 2 teaspoons

1 teaspoon superfine sugar

2 lb cockles or small clams

4 tablespoons extra-virgin olive oil

4 oz slice of Serrano ham or pancetta,
   cut into small dice

2 garlic cloves, finely chopped

1 tablespoon chopped flat-leaf parsley

sea salt and freshly ground black pepper

Working with one artichoke at a time, cut off the top half and then snap off the outer leaves until you reach the softer, pale pink and green leaves on the inside. Peel the stalk with a potato peeler, cut it into quarters lengthwise, and slice the hairy choke off the center with a small sharp knife. Drop into a bowl of water acidulated with all but the 2 teaspoons of lemon juice as you prepare each one. When they are prepared, drop them into boiling salted water with the sugar, bring back to a boil, and cook for about 2–3 minutes until just tender. Drain, refresh under cold water, and leave to drain well on paper towels.

Heat a large pan over high heat. Add the cockles or clams and 5 fl oz water, cover, and cook over high heat for about 30 seconds for cockles, or 3 minutes for clams, uncovering and stirring once or twice, until they have all opened. Drain in a colander and when they are cool enough to handle, remove the meat from the shells.

Heat 3 tablespoons of the olive oil in a frying pan, add the artichoke pieces in a single layer, and fry for 3–4 minutes, seasoning them as they cook, until they are lightly golden on each side. Lift out with a slotted spoon onto a plate. Add the remaining oil and the ham or pancetta to the pan, and fry briefly for about 30 seconds until golden. Reduce the heat, add the garlic, and leave to sizzle for a few seconds. Add the artichokes and cockles or clams to the pan, and toss over medium heat to warm through. Add the remaining lemon juice, the parsley, and some seasoning to taste, toss together briefly and serve.

Sardine empanada

A fish *empanada* has to be one of my all-time favorite snacks. Served warm from the oven with an ice-cold beer, a piece of one of these pies is heaven for me. Please use fresh sardines for this dish. Though it is also extremely good made with good-quality canned tuna steak, or the tuna confit on page 158: simply drain the excess oil from the tuna, flake the fish into large pieces and scatter it over the sauce, with a few thinly sliced green olives or some shredded piquillo peppers if you wish. Eat on the day you make them. Another great and easy empanada is the recipe from my sister-in-law Maria José, which uses smoked salmon, onion and bacon.

Makes 10–12

For the dough

½ cup milk

½ teaspoon superfine sugar

2 teaspoons active dry yeast

1 large egg

scant ¼ stick butter, melted

1⅓ cups all-purpose flour, plus extra
   for dusting

1 teaspoon salt

beaten egg, for glazing

For the filling

6 tablespoons olive oil, plus extra for greasing

3 large onions, halved and thinly sliced

3 garlic cloves, crushed

14 oz vine-ripened tomatoes, skinned
   and chopped

½ teaspoon sugar

21 oz small fresh sardines

sea salt and freshly ground black pepper

To make the dough, warm the milk slightly in a small pan. Pour into a bowl, whisk in the sugar and yeast, and set aside somewhere warm for 15 minutes until foamy. Whisk in the egg and melted butter. Sift the flour and salt into another bowl, add the yeast mixture, and gradually blend the two together to form a soft dough. Turn out onto a lightly floured surface, and knead until smooth. Put the dough into a clean bowl, cover with plastic wrap and leave in a warm place for about 1 hour until doubled in size.

Meanwhile, make the filling. Heat the olive oil in a frying pan, add the onions and garlic, cover and leave to cook gently, stirring now and then, for 15 minutes until the onions are very soft and slightly caramelized. Add the tomatoes and sugar, and simmer for 20–25 minutes until the mixture has reduced and thickened. Season to taste, and set aside to cool.

Next, prepare the sardines. Gut them if necessary, then rinse them under the cold faucet, rubbing off their scales with your thumb and snipping off the fins. Working with one fish at a time, cut off the head and slit open the belly cavity down to the tail. Open the fish out flat, and place it skin-side up on a board. Press firmly along the backbone of the fish with the heel of your hand, then turn it over and pull out the backbone, cutting away the tail and any remaining bone. Check the fish fillet for any stray bones and remove them, then season on both sides with salt and pepper.

Preheat the oven to 400°F. Lightly oil an 8 x 12-inch shallow rectangular baking pan. Punch down the bread dough, turn it out again onto a lightly floured work surface and knead until smooth. Then cut it in half, making one piece slightly larger than the other (approx. 10 oz). Roll out the larger piece thinly, and use to line the base and sides of the prepared pan, leaving the edges overhanging slightly.

Spread half of the onion and tomato sauce over the dough and arrange the opened-out sardines in a single layer on top. Cover with the remaining sauce. Roll out the second piece of dough to the same size as the baking pan and lay it on the filling. Brush the top with beaten egg, then fold the overhanging dough back over the top of the pie, and press the edges together well to form a good seal. Pierce the top of the dough here and there with a fork to allow the steam to escape, and bake for 30 minutes until crisp and golden brown. Remove from the oven and leave to cool in the pan on a wire rack. Cut lengthwise in half and then crosswise to make 10–12 pieces. Serve slightly warm, or at room temperature.

Roasted red pepper and anchovy salad on roasted garlic toasts

The red peppers in Spain are outstanding and there is almost nothing better than peppers roasted in a proper wood-fired oven, a service that during my childhood was provided by the village baker. I'll always remember the aroma that filled the house when my mother returned from the baker's bearing a large tray of these wonderful vegetables. The combination of sweet roasted red peppers and salty anchovies is always a winner. This can be served as a tapas, as the larger Basque-style pintxos or even as a light lunch with a dressed green salad and a poached egg. If you're in a hurry, instead of roasting the red peppers, use a jar/can of Piquillo peppers, which are already roasted and skinned, and have a great smoky flavor.

Serves 4

2 large heads of garlic, unpeeled, plus
   1 fat clove, finely chopped

4 large thyme sprigs

1½ tablespoons extra-virgin olive oil

4 large red bell peppers

2 tablespoons sherry vinegar

8 small slices of rustic white bread,
   about ½-inch thick

16 good-quality anchovy fillets in olive oil,
   drained

sea salt and freshly ground black pepper

Preheat the oven to 400°F. Remove the outer papery skin from each head of garlic and take a thin slice off the top of each one to expose the cloves. Tear off a large square of foil, place the heads of garlic in the center, add 2 of the thyme sprigs, drizzle each head with 1 teaspoon of the olive oil, and sprinkle with a little salt. Wrap securely in the foil, place in a small roasting pan along with the peppers, and roast on the top shelf of the oven for 20–30 minutes, turning the peppers once or twice until the skins have blackened in places. Remove the peppers from the pan, drop them into a plastic bag and leave until cool enough to handle. Return the garlic parcels to the oven and roast for another 35 minutes, or until the cloves feel very soft when pressed.

Meanwhile, slit open the peppers, working over a bowl so that you catch all the juices, and remove and discard the stalks, seeds and skin. Tear the flesh into ½-inch-wide strips, and add to the bowl of juices with the chopped garlic clove, vinegar, the remaining thyme leaves, and the rest of the olive oil. Stir well together.

Remove the garlic from the oven and set the parcel aside. Toast the slices of bread. (I like to put mine on the bars of a preheated cast-iron ridged griddle long enough to give the bread a slightly smoky taste, then finish it off in the toaster.) Unwrap the roasted garlic, squeeze some of the purée from each clove and spread it onto the toast while both are still hot. Sprinkle with a few sea salt flakes and some black pepper. Season the pepper strips with a little salt to taste and spoon onto the garlic toast. Garnish each slice with the anchovy fillets, drizzle over some of the pepper juices, and serve while the toast is still crisp.

Griddled scallops with cauliflower purée and chorizo oil

The northwestern region of Galicia is bordered on two sides by the Atlantic Ocean, so it is not surprising that the cuisine of the area is greatly influenced by the sea. The Rias Bajas provide the perfect conditions for farming scallops, and produce some of the highest-quality scallops in the world. The scallop shell is also the symbol of the town of Santiago de Compostella, the destination of pilgrims from around the world. Every year I promise myself I will make the effort to do the walk, but, as with the London marathon, I never quite get around to doing it! This dish is not traditional in the area, and some people might think it more French than Spanish, but I love the combination of flavors—the cauliflower and the spicy chorizo go so well with the sweetness of the caramelized scallops. You must try the cauliflower from Calahorra once in your life as they have an exceptional, sweet flavor.

Serves 4

2½ cups whole milk
10 oz cauliflower florets (about ½ medium cauliflower)
3 tablespoons extra-virgin olive oil
2 oz cooking chorizo sausage, skinned and finely chopped
1 teaspoon sherry vinegar
1 teaspoon chopped flat-leaf parsley
12 large prepared scallops
sea salt and freshly ground white pepper

Bring the milk to a boil in a large pan. Add the cauliflower florets and 1 teaspoon salt, return to a boil, and cook for 7 minutes until tender. Drain well, reserving the milk. Put the cauliflower into a food processor with 3 tablespoons of the milk and 2 teaspoons of the oil, and blend to a smooth purée. Season to taste with salt and pepper, transfer to a small pan and set aside over low heat to warm through.

Heat 4 teaspoons of olive oil in a small frying pan over medium heat. Add the chopped chorizo, and fry it gently for 1 minute until just golden brown. Stir in the vinegar, parsley and a pinch of sea salt. Keep warm.

Heat a nonstick frying pan over high heat. Rub the scallops with the remaining oil, add them to the pan, and sear for 2 minutes on each side, seasoning them as they cook.

To serve, spoon some of the cauliflower purée onto 4 warmed plates, and arrange the scallops alongside. Spoon over some of the chorizo oil and serve.

Seared scallops and black pudding on crisp potatoes with romesco sauce

To cook and eat a truly fresh scallop is one of the most wonderful culinary experiences imaginable. Whenever possible, try to buy scallops that are freshly opened and sold on the shell, with their corals still attached. They then caramelize beautifully, which helps to enhance the sweetness of the meat. Don't buy scallops in plastic containers as they may be three weeks old.

Serves 4

1 quantity Romesco Sauce (see page 228)

1 lb small, waxy potatoes, peeled and cut into ¼-inch-thick slices

2–3 tablespoons extra-virgin olive oil

leaves from 1 fresh thyme sprig

12 large prepared scallops

2 x 3½-oz smoked morcilla or 7-oz piece of blood sausage, cut into ¼-inch-thick slices

sea salt and freshly ground black pepper

Make the romesco sauce and chill. Put the sliced potatoes into a pan of cold, salted water, bring to a boil and simmer for 5 minutes, or until just tender. Drain well, leave until the steam has died down, then transfer them to a bowl and toss with 1 tablespoon of the oil, the thyme leaves, and some salt and pepper. Preheat the oven to 325°F.

Heat a ridged cast-iron griddle over high heat. Reduce the heat to medium, add half the potato slices in one layer and griddle for about 3 minutes on each side until crisp and golden. Lift them onto a baking sheet, and put in the oven to keep hot. Repeat with the remaining potatoes.

Rub the scallops with a little oil. Heat 2 large nonstick frying pans over high heat, and as soon as they are hot, add the scallops to one pan and sear them for 2 minutes on each side, seasoning them as they cook. Add 1 tablespoon of the oil and the morcilla/blood sausage to the other, and fry for 1 minute on each side. Remove both to a plate. To serve, overlap the crisp potatoes in the center of each of 4 warmed plates and arrange the scallops and blood sausage on top. Spoon some romesco sauce on one side of the plate and serve.

Grilled octopus with olive oil mash

I may be biased, but I think the best octopus in the world comes from Galicia and Spain's northern coastline. I think it has something to do with the cold waters there, and possibly the local species. Octopus is firm, white, and meaty with an almost gelatinous texture, which becomes meltingly tender on cooking. However, I like to cook it so that it remains a little firmer than is usual in Spain. You will only need one-half of the octopus, so cut in half while still frozen and use the other half for another dish (see page 35).

Serves 4

One-half of a 2¾ lb frozen Spanish octopus, defrosted overnight

5 tablespoons extra-virgin olive oil

3 garlic cloves, thinly sliced

1 teaspoon sweet paprika

1 teaspoon red wine vinegar

sea salt and freshly ground black pepper

For the olive oil mashed potatoes

2 lb floury potatoes, such as Russet

4 garlic cloves, peeled, but left whole

1 bay leaf

6 tablespoons extra-virgin olive oil

Cook the octopus according to the instructions on page 35. Shortly before the octopus is ready, make the mashed potatoes. Peel the potatoes and cut them into small chunks. Put into a pan of salted water with the garlic cloves, bay leaf, and 2 tablespoons of the oil. Bring to a boil and simmer for 15–20 minutes until the potatoes are tender.

Remove the octopus from the pan, and when it is cool enough to handle, cut the tentacles away from the head, separate them, then put the pieces onto a lightly oiled baking sheet, and brush with 1 tablespoon of the oil.

Once the potatoes are cooked, drain them in a colander set over a bowl to collect the cooking liquid. Remove and discard the garlic and the bay leaf, return the potatoes to the pan and mash until smooth. Skim the oil from the surface of the cooking water and stir into the potatoes with the remaining oil, some seasoning to taste, and enough of the cooking liquid to give you a smooth, creamy mash. Cover and keep warm over low heat.

Heat a ridged cast-iron griddle over high heat until smoking, then reduce the heat to medium. Brush it with a little oil, add the octopus pieces, and griddle them for 2 minutes on each side until lightly golden. Meanwhile, put the remaining oil into a small pan with the sliced garlic. Place over medium-low heat, and as soon as the garlic is sizzling and has lightly colored, remove from the heat and add the paprika and vinegar.

Spoon the mashed potatoes onto 4 warmed plates and top with the grilled octopus. Spoon over some of the garlic and paprika oil, scatter with a little sea salt and serve.

Salpicón de mariscos

Salpicon, a fish and vegetable salad dressed with vinegar and olive oil, is found in tapas bars throughout the north. The choice of seafood is up to you, but for me the combination should always include shrimp, octopus, and mussels. It's not very common to use cilantro, but it goes so well in this salad. This recipe makes a lot, so serve it when you're entertaining. You can keep it marinated in the vinaigrette for the next day—just add the cilantro at the last minute. Dunking the octopus prevents the tentacles from twisting together, and the pink skin from tearing. This recipe uses only half the octopus, so keep the other half frozen for another dish (see page 33).

Serves 10–12

1 large onion, halved
2 large carrots, sliced
4 fresh bay leaves
½ teaspoon black peppercorns
One-half of a 2¾ lb frozen Spanish octopus, defrosted overnight
5 fl oz extra-virgin olive oil
14 oz (approx 14) large raw unpeeled shrimp
12–16 razor clams, depending on their size
9 oz prepared squid
½ teaspoon crushed dried red pepper flakes
3 garlic cloves, finely chopped
1 lb large mussels, cleaned
finely grated zest of 1 small lemon and 3 tablespoons lemon juice
1 medium-hot red chili pepper, seeded and finely chopped
1 small red onion, halved and thinly sliced
2 scallions, thinly sliced
½ large red romano pepper, thinly sliced
bunch of fresh cilantro, roughly chopped
sea salt and freshly ground black pepper

Bring 8 quarts of water to a boil in a large pan with the onion, carrots, bay leaves, and peppercorns. Holding the head of the octopus between 2 forks, dunk it into the hot water, leave it for a few seconds, then lift it out and bring the water back to a boil. Dunk it once more and remove, bring the water back to a boil, return the octopus to the pan and make sure it is fully submerged. Cover and leave to simmer for 50 minutes–1 hour or until tender. If a skewer inserted into the thickest part of the tentacle goes in easily, it is done. Lift out the octopus and leave until cool enough to handle.

Preheat the broiler to high. Cut the tentacles from the head and separate them. Put onto a baking sheet and brush with a little oil. Broil for 2 minutes on each side until lightly golden. Remove and leave to cool, then cut the tentacles on the diagonal into thin slices and the head into similar-sized pieces. Heat 1 tablespoon of the oil in a large frying pan over medium-high heat, add the shrimp and fry for 1 minute on each side until cooked through. Leave to cool, then peel, discarding the heads and shells, and cut them in half lengthwise and then in half again crosswise.

Return the frying pan to high heat. Add another 2 tablespoons of oil and half the razor clams, hinge-side down. As soon as they have opened, turn them over and cook for about 1 minute until lightly browned and cooked through. Remove and repeat with the remaining clams. Leave them to go cold, then remove the meat from the shells and cut each one into 3 pieces.

Slice the squid crosswise into rings, and each bunch of tentacles in half if large. Heat another tablespoon of oil in the frying pan, add the squid, and stir-fry for 2 minutes until cooked through and lightly browned, adding the crushed dried red pepper flakes, half the chopped garlic and some seasoning after about 1 minute. Spoon onto a plate and allow to cool.

For the mussels, heat a large saucepan over high heat. Add the mussels and 4 tablespoons water, cover and cook for 2–3 minutes, shaking the pan now and then until they have all just opened. Drain and leave until cool enough to handle. Remove the meat from the shells.

Whisk the remaining oil and lemon juice together with the lemon zest, chopped chili pepper, and remaining chopped garlic, and season to taste. Mix the seafood together in a bowl with the red onion and romano pepper, then stir in the dressing. Just before serving, stir in the cilantro, and a little more seasoning to taste. Serve at room temperature.

Crab and shrimp croquetas

In my bar *José* and restaurant *Pizarro*, we love to change the croquetas recipe every day because we have so many regulars. The most popular used to be the Ibérico ham, until they tried the crab and basil—this recipe is the latest addition to the menu, with some shrimp to add flavor and texture.

Serves 6–8 (makes approx. 30)

2 cups whole milk

5 fl oz chicken or vegetable stock

¾ stick butter

generous ¾ cup all-purpose flour

4 oz fresh white crabmeat

4 oz cooked peeled shrimp, finely chopped

1 tablespoon chopped flat-leaf parsley

2 extra-large eggs, beaten

3½ cups bread crumbs, made from stale, crustless white bread

olive oil, for deep-frying

sea salt and freshly ground white pepper

Put the milk and stock in a saucepan and bring to a boil. Melt the butter in another pan over low heat, stir in the flour and cook gently, breaking up the mixture with a wooden spoon as it cooks, for 5 minutes, without letting it brown.

Very gradually beat in the milk and stock, beating really well between each addition, so that the mixture becomes silky smooth. Increase the heat very slightly, and cook gently, stirring constantly, for 5–7 minutes, to cook the flour.

Remove the pan from the heat and stir in the crabmeat, shrimp, parsley, plenty of salt, and a little white pepper to taste. Transfer the mixture to a shallow dish, spread out in an even layer, and press a sheet of plastic wrap onto the surface. Allow to cool, then chill for 2 hours or overnight.

Put the beaten eggs and bread crumbs into separate shallow dishes. Lightly oil your palms and roll 1½ tablespoons of the chilled mixture into balls and then form into zeppelin-shaped barrels. You should make about 30. Refrigerate again for 15–30 minutes.

Heat some oil for deep-frying to 375°F. Dip the croquetas 4–5 at a time into the beaten egg and then the bread crumbs, and deep-fry for 2 minutes until crisp and lightly golden. Transfer to drain briefly on plenty of paper towels while you cook the rest. Serve hot.

Salmon en papillote on spinach with warm tomato and anchovy dressing

Cooking en papillote (in a paper parcel) is a perfect way to cook fish, ensuring it stays beautifully moist. I love to serve it with new potatoes. Try this dish with sea bass too.

Serves 4

4 tablespoons olive oil, plus extra
   for brushing

leaves from 4 thyme sprigs

4 garlic cloves, thinly sliced

4 x 6 oz thick fillets of salmon or
   sea trout, unskinned

1 lb baby leaf spinach, washed

sea salt and freshly ground black pepper

For the tomato and anchovy dressing

6 tablespoons extra-virgin olive oil

2 tablespoons lemon juice

1 large vine-ripened tomato, skinned, seeded
   and cut into small dice

3 anchovy fillets in oil, drained and thinly sliced

1 garlic clove, finely chopped

2 teaspoons small capers, drained and rinsed

2 teaspoons chopped flat-leaf parsley

Preheat the oven to 475°F. Cut out 4 squares of foil and 4 of parchment paper, each 15 inches square. Put the foil squares on top of the paper ones, fold in half, then open up again and brush the centers with olive oil. Scatter the thyme leaves and garlic slices to one side of the crease of each one. Season the fish fillets on both sides with salt and pepper, place on top of the thyme and garlic and drizzle 1 teaspoon of the oil over each piece of fish. Bring the other side of the square over the top of the fish so that the edges meet, then seal by folding over about ½ inch of the edge, about 1½ inches at a time. Work your way all around the edge to make a semicircular, airtight parcel. Put the parcels onto a baking sheet and bake for 8 minutes.

Meanwhile, for the dressing, put the oil, lemon juice, tomato, anchovies, garlic, capers, and some sea salt and pepper to taste into a small pan.

Shortly before the fish is cooked, heat 2 tablespoons of the oil in a large pan. Add the spinach, a large handful at a time, stirring until it just begins to wilt before adding another handful. When all the spinach has wilted, put into a colander, gently press out the excess liquid, then return to the pan with the remaining oil and some seasoning, and stir briefly to heat through. Place the pan of dressing over low heat just to warm through.

Remove the parcels from the oven and slit them open with a sharp knife. Spoon the spinach into the center of 4 warmed plates, and place a piece of fish on top. Stir the parsley into the vinaigrette, spoon it over and around each portion and serve.

Pan-fried sea trout with sautéed summer vegetables

This is one of my favorite supper dishes. I can't wait for the first sea trout to appear at the local fish shop. Although it is rarely seen in Spain, salmon, which is caught regularly in the rivers of Asturias and Cantabria, makes a perfect alternative.

Serves 4

14 oz podded fresh fava beans
8 baby carrots, halved lengthwise
3½ oz fine green beans, halved
20 asparagus tips, halved lengthwise
3½ tablespoons olive oil
½ cup shallots, thinly sliced
2 garlic cloves, thinly sliced
4 x 6 oz thick fillets of sea trout, unskinned
2 tablespoons chopped fresh tarragon
sea salt and freshly ground black pepper

Bring a large pan of salted water to a boil. Add the fava beans, cook for 4 minutes, then remove with a slotted spoon and drop into a bowl of ice-cold water. Add the carrots to the boiling water with the green beans and cook for 2 minutes. Drop in the asparagus tips and cook for another 2 minutes, then drain and add to the bowl of ice water. When they are cold, drain and dry well on paper towels. Skin the fava beans.

Heat 2 tablespoons of the olive oil in a large frying pan, add the shallots and garlic and cook gently until soft, but not brown. Set aside.

Rub the sea trout with a little olive oil and season. Heat an ovenproof frying pan over medium heat, add ½ tablespoon of the oil, then the sea trout, skin-side down, and fry gently for 4–5 minutes until the skin is crisp and golden. Carefully flip the pieces over and cook for another 2 minutes. Set aside. The fish will continue to cook in the heat of the pan.

Heat another frying pan over medium heat, add the remaining oil and the vegetables and toss together gently until heated through. Add the chopped tarragon and a little seasoning. Spoon the vegetables onto warmed plates, put the pieces of fish on top and serve.

Broiled cod with fava bean and mint purée, and pancetta

It is quite rare to see fresh cod in Spain, but since I moved to the UK, I love tucking in to fish and chips now and then, with mushy peas. This dish is based on similar flavors, but instead of dried peas, uses fresh lima beans flavored with a little mint, and has the addition of crisp, salty pancetta.

Serves 4

4 x 6 oz thick fillets of cod, unskinned

12 thin slices of pancetta or smoked bacon

sea salt and freshly ground black pepper

For the fava bean purée

4 tablespoons extra-virgin olive oil, plus extra for drizzling

¾ cup shallots, finely chopped

2 garlic cloves, crushed

21 oz fresh fava beans, podded

2 tablespoons chopped mint

Heat 2 tablespoons of the oil in a small pan. Add the shallots and garlic, and cook gently for 5 minutes until soft, but not browned.

Preheat the broiler to high. Drop the beans into a pan of salted boiling water, and cook for 3 minutes, or until tender. Drain well, remove the skins, then put into a food processor, and add a tablespoon of the olive oil, the cooked shallots and garlic, and the mint. Process until smooth, then transfer to a small pan and set aside.

Rub the pieces of cod with a little of the remaining olive oil and season with salt and pepper. Place skin-side up on a lightly oiled baking pan or the rack of the broiler pan and broil for 6–8 minutes, until just cooked.

Just before the cod is ready, reheat the bean purée and season. Heat a large nonstick frying pan over medium-high heat. Add 1 teaspoon of the oil and the slices of pancetta, side by side, and fry for 1 minute on each side until crisp and golden. Lift onto paper towels to drain. Spoon the bean purée onto warmed plates, and place the cod on top, skin-side up. Rest the pancetta up against the cod, drizzle with a little olive oil, add a sprinkling of sea salt and a little crushed black pepper, and serve.

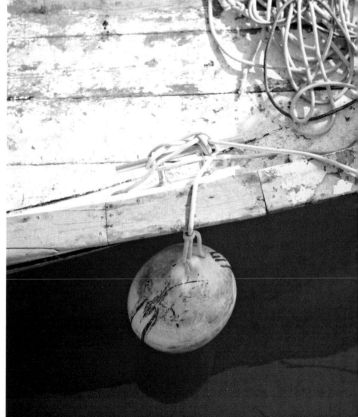

Pan-fried hake with cockles, asparagus, peas, and mint

Hake is not as loved in America as it is in Spain. More common fish include hailbut or cod, both of which can be substituted here. A similar dish to this one is very popular in the North, using clams and parsley instead of cockles and mint, but this is my interpretation.

Serves 4

7 oz fine asparagus tips, cut into 1-inch lengths
1 cup petits pois, freshly podded or frozen
3–4 tablespoons olive oil
1 cup shallots, finely chopped
3 garlic cloves, finely chopped
4 x 7 oz thick fillets of hake, unskinned
1 lb cockles or small clams, cleaned
½ cup fish or chicken stock
½ tablespoon chopped parsley
½ tablespoon chopped mint
sea salt and freshly ground black pepper

Drop the asparagus into a pan of boiling salted water and cook for 1½ minutes. Add the peas, cook for another 30 seconds or so until both the vegetables are just tender, then drain. Refresh under cold water and set aside.

Heat 1½ tablespoons of the oil in a large saucepan, add the shallots and garlic, and cook gently for 4–5 minutes until very soft but not browned. Remove from the heat.

Rub the outside of the fish fillets generously with oil and season with salt and pepper. Heat a nonstick frying pan over medium-high heat, add the hake skin-side down, and fry for 2½ minutes, or until the skin is crisp and golden. Turn the fish over, reduce the heat slightly, and continue to fry for 4 minutes until cooked through.

Meanwhile, return the pan of softened shallots and garlic to high heat and, as soon as it is hot, add the cockles or clams, and fish or chicken stock, cover, and cook, shaking the pan now and then, for 2–3 minutes until the cockles or clams have opened. Uncover, and stir in the asparagus, peas, parsley, mint, and some seasoning to taste.

Lift each piece of hake onto large, warmed soup plates, spoon some of the cockle or clam mixture over and around the fish, together with the juices, and serve.

Bacalao à la romana with anchovies and a green salad

For good *bacalao* (dried salt cod) the fish should be white, not at all gray or yellow, and smell sweetly of the sea even though it will have been out of the water for a long time. When I want to serve *bacalao* as a main course, I prefer to use a cut called *lomo*, which are square-shaped portion-sized pieces of fish cut from the thicker end of the fillet, but for fritters, for example, where the fish is flaked into small pieces, the tail end cut is fine. Make sure that you soak it for just long enough to get rid of the excess salt, but not for so long that it loses its characteristic taste.

Serves 4

4 x 5 oz pieces of thick bacalao
　(dried salt cod)

1 large soft lettuce

olive oil, for shallow-frying

flour, for coating

2 extra large free-range (cage-free) eggs,
　beaten

large pinch of sweet paprika, to garnish

sea salt and freshly ground black pepper

8 good-quality anchovy fillets in olive oil,
　to serve

For the anchovy vinaigrette

2 good-quality anchovy fillets in olive oil,
　drained

1 tablespoon sherry vinegar

4 tablespoons extra-virgin olive oil

Knock the excess salt off the cod and place it, skin-side up, in a bowl. Cover with plenty of cold water, and leave to soak for 24 hours, changing the water every 6 hours or so. After this time, take a small piece of fish from the thickest part and taste it. If it doesn't taste too salty, it's ready to use, but remember, salt cod needs to be a little bit salty, and also it will taste slightly more salty once it is cooked.

Drain the pieces of salt cod and leave them to dry well on plenty of paper towels. It is important to get rid of all the water, so press down lightly on the top of each piece to help remove any excess.

For the salad, remove and discard the outer leaves from the lettuce and break the rest into separate leaves. Wash and dry well, and put into a large salad bowl.

To make the anchovy vinaigrette, put the anchovy fillets into a mortar or a small bow,l and pound to a paste. Stir in the vinegar, gradually whisk in the extra-virgin olive oil, and season to taste with salt and pepper.

Pour ½ inch of olive oil in a large nonstick frying pan, place over medium heat until approximately 325°F (use a cooking thermometer). Coat the pieces of salt cod in flour, knock off the excess, then coat well in the beaten egg. Lower into the hot oil and fry for 4–4½ minutes on each side, depending on the thickness of the fish, until it is cooked through and richly golden brown. Lift onto some paper towels, leave to drain briefly, then transfer to serving plates. Toss the anchovy vinaigrette through the lettuce leaves and pile alongside the fish. Arrange the anchovy fillets on one side, sprinkle each piece of fish and the plate with a little paprika, and serve.

Bacalao fritters with alioli

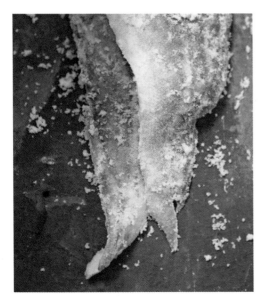

This recipe comes from my friend Aitor, one of the greatest young chefs that I know. I can't resist making these fritters every time I have a party, and serving them with plenty of alioli on the side for dipping or just with some lemon juice. Enjoy them as soon as they are cooked, while they are puffed up, crisp and golden, and piping hot.

Serves 8 (makes approx. 30 fritters)

9 oz bacalao (dried salt cod)

7 oz floury potatoes, cut into small chunks

sunflower or inexpensive olive oil, for
  deep-frying

1 tablespoon extra-virgin olive oil

1 garlic clove, crushed

4 tablespoons flour

1 extra large free-range (cage-free) egg,
  beaten

2 tablespoons chopped flat-leaf parsley

sea salt and freshly ground black pepper

1 quantity Alioli (garlic mayonnaise, see
  page 227), or lemon wedges, to serve

Knock the excess salt off the cod and place it, skin-side up, in a bowl. Cover with plenty of cold water and leave to soak for 24 hours, changing the water every 6 hours or so. After this time, take a small piece of fish from the thickest part and taste it. If it doesn't taste too salty, it's ready to use, but remember: salt cod needs to be a little bit salty, and also it will taste slightly more salty once it is cooked.

Put the salt cod into a pan with 2½ cups cold water. Bring to a boil over medium heat, turn off the heat and leave for 10 minutes. Lift the fish onto a plate with a fish spatula and leave to cool. Add the potatoes to the water, bring back to a boil, and simmer for 10 minutes until tender. Drain, reserving the cooking water, return them to the pan and mash until smooth. Flake the salt cod into a bowl, discarding the skin and any bones, and coarsely mash with the end of a rolling pin (or use a large mortar and pestle if you have one).

Heat the oil for deep-frying to 350°F. Meanwhile, warm the olive oil and garlic in a medium pan. As soon as the garlic is sizzling, add 5 fl oz of the reserved cooking water and bring to a boil. Add the flour, reduce the heat to low, and beat vigorously until the mixture is smooth and thickens slightly. Remove from the heat, leave to cool slightly, then gradually beat in the beaten egg to make a smooth paste. Stir in the mashed potatoes, salt cod, chopped parsley, and a little salt and pepper to taste.

Drop 6–8 heaping teaspoons of the mixture, spaced well apart, into the hot oil and cook for 4 minutes, turning them over halfway through, until they are crisp and golden. Drain each batch briefly on paper towels while you cook the rest. Serve hot with alioli or lemon wedges for squeezing.

Chicken in beer

The smell of this dish cooking reminds me of home, and my mother's cooking, but of course my mother never used mustard and butter in her recipe. She would always serve it with *patatas fritas* (French fries), but it would also be good with Olive Oil Mashed Potatoes (see page 33).

Serves 4

1 x 3¼ lb chicken, cut into 8 and skinned

1 teaspoon sweet paprika

3 tablespoons flour

3 tablespoons olive oil

¼ stick butter

1 lb onions, halved and thinly sliced

6 whole cloves

1 teaspoon fennel seeds

1 tablespoon sugar

4 fresh bay leaves

2 teaspoons Dijon mustard

1 cup lager-style beer

1 cup chicken stock

2 teaspoons red wine vinegar

sea salt and freshly ground black pepper

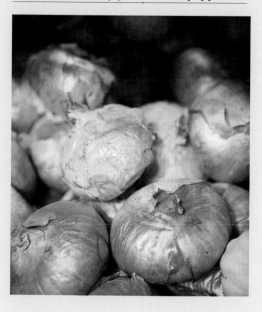

Sprinkle the pieces of chicken all over with the paprika, ½ teaspoon salt, and some black pepper. Then coat in the flour and knock off the excess. Heat the olive oil in a flameproof casserole. Add the chicken pieces to the casserole, and fry for about 4 minutes on each side until golden brown. Lift out onto a plate and set aside.

Melt the butter in the casserole, then add the onions, cloves, fennel seeds, 2 teaspoons of the sugar, the bay leaves, and some salt and pepper. Cover and fry over medium heat, stirring now and then, for 15 minutes, until the onions are soft and nicely caramelized.

Uncover, and stir in the remaining sugar and the mustard, then the beer, chicken stock, and 1 teaspoon of the vinegar. Return the chicken pieces to the pan, bring to a boil, cover, and simmer for 30 minutes until the sauce has thickened, and the chicken is tender. Uncover, and stir in the remaining vinegar and some salt and pepper to taste. Serve hot.

Carpaccio of veal with baby fava beans and lemon

The beef from this region is famous all over Spain. The value placed on dairy and beef cattle means herds are jealously guarded and meticulously cared for, grazing on lush pasture most of the year. The meat is sold according to age at slaughter: *ternera* (veal), at a maximum of 10 months old, is very popular and either sliced very thin and fried briefly or roasted; *anojo* is 10–18 months old; and *cebon*, 18–30 months old, is marbled with fat and full of flavor. I like to use veal rather than beef for carpaccio as the flavor is more delicate, and the color looks beautiful on the plate.

Serves 6

9 oz piece of veal loin

12 oz small podded fresh fava beans

For the dressing

1 tablespoon lemon juice

1 teaspoon Dijon mustard

4 tablespoons extra-virgin olive oil

2 teaspoons chopped mint

sea salt and freshly ground black pepper

To garnish

3–4 small mint leaves, finely shredded

small piece of cured Manchego cheese

Wrap the loin of veal tightly in plastic wrap to form a cylindrical shape and freeze for 2 hours, or until it becomes firm enough to slice.

Meanwhile, drop the fava beans into a pan of boiling salted water and cook for 3 minutes until just tender. Drain, and refresh under cold water, then pop the bright green beans out of their skins into a bowl.

Make a slightly thick dressing by whisking the lemon juice and mustard together, then gradually whisking in the oil, and some salt and pepper to taste.

Remove the veal from the freezer, and with the plastic wrap still in place, cut it into very thin slices. Remove the pieces of plastic wrap, and arrange the slices, slightly overlapping, over the base of 4 large plates.

Stir the chopped mint into the dressing. Stir 1 tablespoon of the dressing into the fava beans and adjust the seasoning if necessary. Drizzle the remaining dressing over the veal, then scatter the fava beans over the top. Sprinkle with the shredded mint, then use a sharp vegetable peeler to shave the Manchego cheese over each portion. Serve immediately.

Veal chops with black-eyed peas, pancetta, and cabbage

Asadors (simple restaurants where you can enjoy the local food, and probably a glass of cider) are very popular in northern Spain. *Chuleton* (a large beef rib chop) is often used, but thick cut veal chops in my opinion are just as good. The peas and cabbage that accompany this dish celebrate some of the most highly revered ingredients from this region: dried beans and cabbage or *grelos*. *Grelos* are not available outside Spain, but cavolo nero or even curly kale are two very good alternatives.

Serves 4

7 tablespoons extra-virgin olive oil
1 medium onion, finely chopped
¾ teaspoon crushed dried red pepper flakes
11 oz black-eyed peas, soaked overnight in cold water
4 bay leaves
1 tablespoon fennel seeds
1 head of garlic, cloves separated, peeled and finely chopped
leaves from an 7-inch rosemary sprig, finely chopped
4 x 1 lb veal chops, cut about 1-inch thick
5 oz pancetta or smoked bacon cubes, cut into small dice
7 oz cavolo nero leaves or curly kale, torn into small pieces
⅔ cup chicken stock
freshly grated nutmeg
sea salt and freshly ground black pepper

Heat 3 tablespoons of the olive oil in a medium pan, add the onion and ¼ teaspoon of the crushed dried red pepper flakes, cover, and fry gently for 10 minutes until soft. Drain the black-eyed peas, and stir them into the pan with the bay leaves and 3 cups cold water. Bring to a boil, partially cover, and leave to cook over gentle heat for 1¼–1½ hours, stirring occasionally, until the peas are tender, and the liquid has almost disappeared.

While the peas are cooking, lightly crush the fennel seeds (using a mortar and pestle if you have one), then mix in the remaining red pepper flakes, half the chopped garlic, the rosemary, 2 tablespoons of the remaining olive oil, 1 teaspoon sea salt and some freshly ground black pepper. Rub this mixture over both sides of each veal chop and set aside in the fridge for 1 hour.

Heat a ridged or flat cast-iron griddle over high heat. Reduce the heat slightly, add the chops, and cook for 6–8 minutes on each side until cooked through, but still pink and juicy. The temperature at the center of the meat should register 140°F on a meat thermometer. Remove from the griddle to a plate, cover loosely with foil, and leave to rest for 5 minutes.

While the chops are cooking, finish off the peas. By the time they are tender, there should very little liquid remaining—the peas should just be nicely moist. Remove and discard the bay leaves, stir in ½ teaspoon salt, cover, and set aside. Heat the remaining olive oil in a wide shallow pan, add the pancetta or bacon, and fry for 2–3 minutes until lightly golden. Add the remaining garlic, fry for a few seconds, then stir in the cavolo nero or curly kale and stir-fry for 2 minutes until it begins to wilt. Add the chicken stock, cover, and cook over low heat for 8–10 minutes until tender. Stir in the cooked peas, and season to taste with some nutmeg, salt, and pepper. Serve with the veal chops.

Beef, red pepper, and paprika stew

The best beef comes from the north of Spain where it is known as *ternera*. One of the most popular ways of preparing it is simply barbecued over a charcoal fire. Known as a *chilindron* in Spain, this is one of the most famous dishes from Navarra, the Basque Country, and further east, Aragon. A *chilindron* is more traditionally made with lamb, slow-cooked with plenty of dried and fresh red peppers from those regions, but I also love it made with beef. This recipe is just perfect for entertaining when you don't want to spend too much time in the kitchen. In Spain, most stews are served with fried potatoes, but mashed potatoes or rice would be excellent too.

Serves 6

3 dried choricero (or other mild) peppers
1 cup dried wild mushrooms, such as porcini
3¼ lb blade or chuck steak
4–6 tablespoons extra-virgin olive oil
4 oz diced pancetta, bacon, or Serrano ham
2 large onions, chopped
10 garlic cloves, thinly sliced
1 tablespoon sweet paprika
1 tablespoon hot paprika
1¼ cups white wine
14 oz skinned, chopped tomatoes, fresh or canned
1 tablespoon chopped rosemary
4 bay leaves
3 large red bell peppers
sea salt and freshly ground black pepper

Slit open the dried peppers and remove the stalks and seeds. Put them into a small bowl and cover with boiling water. Put the dried mushrooms into another small bowl and cover with ⅔ cup hot water. Leave both to soak for 1 hour. Cut the beef into 1¼-inch chunks, and season well with salt and pepper.

Heat 2 tablespoons of the oil in a flameproof casserole over medium-high heat. Lightly brown the beef in batches, transferring each batch to a bowl once it is done, and adding a little more oil when necessary.

Drain the mushrooms and peppers, reserving the mushroom soaking water. Squeeze out the excess liquid from the mushrooms, and scrape the red pepper flesh away from the skins, discarding the skins. Add another 2 tablespoons of the oil to the casserole along with the pancetta, bacon, or ham, and when it is lightly golden, add the onions. When they are beginning to color, add the garlic and mushrooms, and continue to cook until the onions are soft and lightly golden. Stir in both the sweet and hot paprika and cook for another 2 minutes.

Add the wine to the casserole, and simmer until reduced by half. Return the beef and any juices to the casserole with the tomatoes, rosemary, bay leaves, choricero pepper flesh, ½ teaspoon salt, and some black pepper. Add enough of the mushroom soaking water so that the liquid comes about two-thirds of the way up the beef and stir well. Cover, and simmer gently for about 2½–3 hours, or until the beef is tender.

Meanwhile, grill the red peppers under high heat, turning them occasionally until their skins are quite black. Drop them into a plastic bag and leave to cool, then break them open, and remove the stalks and seeds. Peel off the skin, and cut the flesh into thin strips. Stir into the stew 10 minutes before the end of the cooking time, together with a little more seasoning to taste. Serve the stew hot.

Beef rib chop with fried green peppers

When I was young I would regularly make myself a dish of potatoes and green peppers fried in olive oil, topped with a fried egg, especially mid-morning after a late night out. In the north of Spain *chuleton*, a large beef rib chop, is often served with fried *pimientos de Padrón*, those fiery little green peppers from Galicia, but these can be difficult to get hold of in the US. Long thin Turkish green peppers work particularly well in this dish, or you can use ordinary green peppers: just cut them into quarters lengthwise.

Serves 2–3

4 tablespoons olive oil, plus extra for the beef

8 pimientos de Pardon, deseeded or 8 long Turkish green peppers, seeded and cut into ½-inch-wide strips

3 fat garlic cloves, finely chopped

leaves from a 2½-inch rosemary sprig, finely chopped

large (approx. 3 lb) beef rib chop

sea salt and freshly ground black pepper

Preheat your barbecue to high or place a ridged cast-iron grill pan over high heat. Heat the oil in a large frying pan over medium heat. Add the green peppers and fry for 12–15 minutes, turning regularly, until they are soft and nicely colored. Add the garlic and rosemary and fry for another 1–2 minutes. Season to taste with salt and pepper, and set aside to keep warm.

Meanwhile, rub the beef rib chop with some oil, and season well all over with salt and pepper. Grill the beef for about 6–7 minutes on each side for medium rare, or until the center of the meat registers 130°F on a meat thermometer. Transfer it to a board, cover with foil and leave it to rest for 5 minutes, during which time the internal temperature will rise to 140°F.

To serve, cut the meat away from the bone, and then diagonally, like a steak, into slices. Serve with the fried green peppers and some *patatas fritas* (French fries).

Blue cheese with two apple compotes

I love salty, tangy blue cheese served with a sharp, yet sweet apple compote and here I have given two variations. Allow about 2 oz of cheese per person and serve the compotes at room temperature. Choose a variety of apple that doesn't collapse during cooking. Macintosh and Granny Smith both work well. Membrillo is a paste made from quinces, which is known as the perfect accompaniment to Manchego, but the addition of apple makes it amazing with blue cheese. One of my favorite blue cheeses from Spain is Cabrales from Asturias, which is really strong and pungent and always a winner on a cheeseboard.

Serves 4–6

For the zesty apple and lemon compote

4 large, firm dessert apples, peeled, cored, quartered and cut into large dice

finely grated zest of 1 large lemon and 3 tablespoons lemon juice

2½ tablespoons superfine sugar

For the apple and membrillo compote

½ stick unsalted butter

4 large firm dessert apples, peeled, cored, quartered, and each quarter cut into 3 slices

2 oz *membrillo*, (quince paste) thinly sliced

1 tablespoon light brown sugar

1½–2 tablespoons lemon juice

¼ teaspoon ground cinnamon

2 tablespoons apple juice

To serve

2 oz Picos Blue, La Peral or Cabrales cheese per person

For the zesty apple and lemon compote, mix the apples with the lemon zest and juice, and sugar, cover, and leave to marinate for 30 minutes. Transfer the mixture to a saucepan, place over medium heat, cover, and leave to cook gently for 5 minutes until the apples are just tender. Uncover, increase the heat slightly, and cook for another 4–5 minutes, or until the excess liquid has evaporated. Remove and leave to cool.

For the compote, melt the butter in a large, nonstick frying pan, add the apple slices in a single layer, and fry gently for 4–5 minutes, turning over halfway through, once they are lightly browned. Lift the slices onto a plate, and pour off the excess butter. Add the membrillo to the pan with the sugar, lemon juice, cinnamon, and apple juice, and cook gently, stirring, until you have a smooth, jam-like sauce. Return the apple slices to the pan, and stir to coat them in the sauce. Remove from the heat and leave to cool. Serve the compotes at room temperature with the cheese.

Baked cheesecakes with blueberries

The north of Spain is renowned for its production of milk, which of course results in plenty of cheese and dairy desserts. We call cheesecakes *quesadillas*. **This recipe is a big seller in Pizarro, where Maria, my pastry chef, changes the fruit according to the season—blueberries in summer, spiced quince in autumn, and caramelized oranges in winter (see page 93).**

Serves 6

1 lb full-fat cream cheese

scant ⅔ cup superfine sugar

1½ tablespoons cornstarch

pinch of salt

2 large eggs

scant ½ cup sour cream

confectioners' sugar, for dusting

For the blueberries

4½ tablespoons lemon juice

6 tablespoons superfine sugar

8 oz blueberries

1 teaspoon arrowroot

Tightly wrap some foil around the base of 6 poaching rings or molds, 2¾ inches wide and 2½ inches deep, then line the base and sides with parchment paper. Place on a baking sheet.

Preheat the oven to 225°F. Put the cream cheese into a bowl, and beat with an electric hand mixer until smooth and creamy. Beat in the sugar, cornstarch, salt, and eggs, then stir in the sour cream. Pour the mixture into the molds and bake for 35–40 minutes until set, but still slightly wobbly in the center. The cheesecakes will continue to firm up as they cool. Remove from the oven, and leave to cool. These can be chilled if you wish, but are best served at room temperature.

For the blueberries, put the lemon juice and sugar into a small pan, and leave over low heat until the sugar has dissolved. Add the blueberries, bring to a gentle simmer, and cook for 1 minute. Mix the arrowroot with 1 teaspoon cold water, stir into the fruit, and cook for about 30 seconds until thickened. Transfer to a small bowl, and allow to cool.

If you chilled the cheesecakes, remove them from the fridge 30 minutes or so before serving. Gently slide them out of their molds, and carefully peel off the lining paper from the bases. Put onto serving plates, and then peel away the strips of paper from the sides. Dust the tops of the cheesecakes with confectioners' sugar, spoon the blueberries around, and serve.

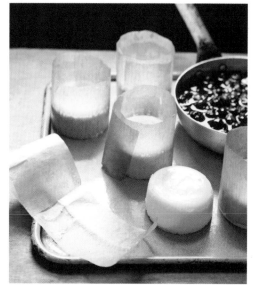

Orange-scented apple buñuelos

Buñuelos are crisp deep-fried fritters, popular all over Spain. I came up with the idea for these one day when I had a few apples to use up, and needed a quick dessert to serve to friends. I have to say they were very well received. I love to serve them with the Crema Catalana Ice Cream on page 61.

Serves 6

For the batter

scant ½ cup whole milk

½ teaspoon superfine sugar

¾ cup all-purpose flour

½ teaspoon active dry yeast

pinch of salt

1 extra large egg, separated

3 tablespoons hard cider

1 tablespoon olive oil

olive or sunflower oil, for deep-frying

For the orange-scented apples

3–4 small dessert apples, such as Mcintosh

finely grated zest of ½ orange

1 tablespoon orange juice

1 tablespoon orange-flavored liqueur, such as Grand Marnier

To finish

¼ cup superfine sugar

1 teaspoon ground cinnamon

For the batter, warm the milk with the superfine sugar. Sift the flour, yeast, and salt into a bowl. Make a well in the center, add the egg yolk and gradually whisk in the milk and cider, followed by the oil to make a smooth batter. Cover with plastic wrap and set aside in a warm place for 1 hour until frothy.

Quarter, core, and peel the apples and cut each piece into 3 wedges. Put them into a bowl with the orange zest, orange juice, and orange liqueur and mix well together. Set aside for 1 hour alongside the batter.

When you are ready to cook the fritters, heat some oil for deep-frying to 350°F. Whisk the egg white in a clean bowl into soft peaks and gently fold into the batter.

Using a fork, lower one piece of apple at a time into the batter so that it takes on a thin, even coating, and then drop it into the hot oil. Cook, 6 pieces at a time, for 3 minutes, turning them over halfway through, until crisp and golden. Remove with a slotted spoon and drain briefly on plenty of paper towels while you cook the remainder.

Mix the superfine sugar with the ground cinnamon, sprinkle over the fritters, and serve immediately, while they are still hot and crisp.

Crema catalana ice cream

Crema catalana **is served all over Spain. Not unlike a crème brulée, though not cooked in the oven, it is an orange-flavored thick custard, traditionally set in a shallow terracotta dish, topped with a thin layer of caramel just before serving. I decided one day to take things a step further by churning the custard in an ice-cream machine and folding some crushed caramel in at the end. It worked really well and makes a lovely accompaniment to the apple fritters on page 58.**

Makes 2¼ cups

scant cup whole milk

1 cinnamon stick

finely grated zest of 1 small lemon

finely grated zest of 1 small orange

4 extra large free-range (cage-free) egg yolks

½ cup superfine sugar

1¼ cups heavy cream

For the caramel

scant ⅔ cup superfine sugar

⅓ cup cold water

Put the milk, cinnamon stick, lemon and orange zest into a saucepan and bring to a boil. Remove from the heat, and set aside for at least 30 minutes to infuse.

Beat the egg yolks and sugar together in a bowl. Bring the milk back to a boil, gradually whisk into the egg-yolk mixture, then strain back into the cleaned-out pan. Cook over gentle heat, stirring constantly, for 3–4 minutes until the mixture thickens, and lightly coats the back of a wooden spoon. Remove from the heat, cool, then stir in the cream and refrigerate overnight.

To make the caramel, line a baking sheet with parchment paper. Put the sugar and cold water into a small pan, and leave over low heat to dissolve. Then bring to a boil, and cook until it turns into a brick-red caramel. Pour the mixture onto the baking sheet, and tilt the sheet back and forth to spread the mixture into a thin, even layer. Leave to get cold, then break into pieces using the handle of a knife.

Either churn the ice-cream mixture in an ice-cream machine, or pour it into a shallow container and freeze until almost solid. Scrape into the bowl of a food processor and blend briefly until smooth, then return to the container, and freeze once more. Repeat this 2–3 times more until the mixture is very smooth. If serving immediately, you can churn some of the caramel pieces into the ice cream. Otherwise, sprinkle over the top just before serving.

THE EAST

THE EAST: INTRODUCTION

Barcelona feels like a second home to me. When I arrive in this city, the first morning I go to the famous Boqueria food market to have breakfast—normally a slice of tortilla and some *pan con tomate* (tomato bread). Whether for work or pleasure, I love my trips to Barcelona and always leave with a great taste in my mouth. I find the entire Catalonia region to be very open-minded and cosmopolitan, yet it also manages to maintain its own language and traditions.

Catalonia is rich in gastronomic delights. Its perfect position between the Pyrenees and the Mediterranean provides a wealth of specialty ingredients. I love to cook with Catalonia's wild mushrooms, shrimps from the port of Palamós, and capers with the olives and oils from the region. And let's not forget the Cava, sparkling white or rosé wine, which I often use in my dishes, as well as serving when there is an excuse to celebrate.

The region of Murcia is another of Spain's market gardens, producing many of the country's vegetables, but in the northwest of Murcia, where four rivers cross a mountainous region, lies Calasparra, which has been growing rice since the 14th century. The quality of Calasparra rice is recognized by its Denominación de Origen status and it is one of my favorites. I use it for my rice dishes, including paella, which is from neighboring Valencia.

Valencia is known throughout the world for paella, vibrantly colored with saffron and paprika and brimming with the best seasonal ingredients of the region and the sea, but there are many other Spanish rice dishes that you have to try. The soupy rice dish and black rice *arroz negro* dish on pages 76 and 77 are both spectacular. Valencia is also the home of my dear friend María José San Román. Everyone knows her as "the queen of the saffron" as she incorporates it so beautifully in her rice dishes. If ever you go to Alicante, you must visit one of her restaurants: Monastrell has a wonderful and ever-changing tasting menu and the Tavern of the Gourmet has a more relaxed atmosphere.

The dried fruits are of excellent quality in these eastern regions; a reminder of Spain's Moorish past that persists in the cuisine, and almonds and hazelnuts are grown for the production of the famous nougat (turrón) from Alicante—a sweet treat that is found on every table in Spain at Christmas time. Nuts, especially blanched almonds, are used in Spanish cuisine to flavor and thicken dishes such as stews and soups, as well as sauces and desserts.

Wild mushroom, watercress, and blue cheese tart

The hills and mountains of Spain provide the perfect growing conditions for wild mushrooms and nowhere do the Spanish love to go picking these delicacies more than in the northeastern regions. There you will find chanterelles, pied bleu, pied de mouton, trompette de la mort, oyster, porcini and saffron milk cap. Wild mushrooms go extremely well with blue cheese and walnuts, so this is my recipe for a tart using all three, which is, by the way, an excellent dish for vegetarians. I always make this for my friend Catriona when she comes over to help me with my website.

Serves 8

11 oz mixed wild mushrooms
2 tablespoons olive oil
1 scant cup watercress leaves
3½ oz Picos Blue cheese, crumbled
1¼ cups heavy cream
4 extra large free-range (cage-free) eggs
sea salt and freshly ground black pepper

For the pastry

½ cup walnut pieces
1¾ cups all-purpose flour, plus extra for dusting
5 tablespoons chilled butter, cut into pieces
4 tablespoons chilled lard, cut into pieces

Preheat the oven to 400°F. For the pastry, spread the walnuts on a baking sheet and roast for 7–8 minutes. Remove, and leave to cool. Put them into a food processor and add a heaping ⅓ cup of the flour. Grind together briefly until the nuts are finely chopped. Add the remaining flour and ½ teaspoon salt, together with the butter and lard, and process briefly once more, until the mixture resembles fine bread crumbs. Transfer the mixture into a bowl and stir in 2 tablespoons cold water until the mixture comes together into a ball, then turn out onto a lightly floured surface, and knead briefly until smooth. Roll out thinly, adding a little more flour to the surface, and use to line a lightly greased loose-based 9-inch 1½-inch deep tart pan. Chill for 20 minutes.

Put a baking sheet on the middle shelf of the oven, and leave it to get hot. Line the pastry case with foil and a thin layer of baking beans, slide it onto the baking sheet and bake for 20 minutes. Remove the foil and beans, and return to the oven for 5 minutes, until the pastry is lightly golden. Remove and set aside while you make the filling. Reduce the oven temperature to 375°F.

Clean the wild mushrooms thoroughly by brushing away any dirt with a dry pastry brush, and wiping them with a damp cloth if necessary. Heat 1 tablespoon of the olive oil in a large frying pan over high heat, add half the mushrooms and some seasoning and fry briskly for 1 minute until they have softened slightly and any excess moisture has evaporated. Transfer to a plate, and repeat with the remainder.

Scatter the mushrooms, watercress leaves, and blue cheese evenly over the base of the pastry case. Beat together the cream and eggs with some seasoning, pour the mixture into the tart pan and return it to the baking sheet. Bake for 30–35 minutes, until set and lightly golden. Serve warm, cut into wedges.

Wild mushroom and Manchego cheese canalóns

Take care to clean the wild mushrooms properly. If picking them yourself, clean them before putting them in your basket so that the dirt doesn't become trapped in the gills. Simply brush them clean with a pastry brush, and wipe them with a slightly damp cloth only if you really have to, but never, ever wash them. Mushrooms are like sponges and absorb water very easily, which will ruin them when you come to cook them. If you are using ready-made pasta for this dish, ensure you find a brand that is rolled out quite thinly. Many are far too thick in my opinion. My mother always makes *canalóns* with ground meat and tomato sauce, but I have to say that my recipe is better than hers!

Serves 8

1 cup dried wild mushrooms, such as porcini

1 tablespoon olive oil

3 tablespoons butter, plus extra for greasing

¾ cup shallots, finely chopped

3 garlic cloves, finely chopped

18 oz mixed fresh wild mushrooms, cleaned and sliced

leaves from 3 large thyme sprigs

3 tablespoons flour

1¼ cups whole milk

freshly grated nutmeg

16 *canaló* wrappers or 8 large sheets fresh lasagne pasta, cut into 4¾ x 6-inch rectangles

3 oz semi-cured Manchego cheese, finely grated

sea salt and freshly ground black pepper

For the béchamel sauce

5 cups whole milk

¾ stick butter

scant ½ cup flour

Put the dried mushrooms into a small bowl and cover with boiling water. Leave to soak for 30 minutes, then drain well, squeezing out all the excess water, and slice thinly. Bring a large pan of salted water to the boil.

Heat the oil and butter in a large frying pan. Add the shallots and garlic, and cook gently for 5 minutes until soft, but not brown. Add the soaked and fresh wild mushrooms, and the thyme, increase the heat to high, and stir-fry for 4–5 minutes, or until all the excess moisture has evaporated and the mushrooms are tender.

Stir the flour into the pan, then gradually stir in the milk. Bring to a boil, stirring, and leave to simmer for 5 minutes, stirring occasionally. Season to taste with nutmeg, salt, and pepper. Allow to cool slightly.

Meanwhile, drop the *canaló* wrappers or lasagne pasta into the pan of hot water, turn off the heat and leave to soak for 5 minutes until just tender. Drain, run under cold water, then quickly separate the wrappers and lay side by side on some plastic wrap. Spoon a generous 2 tablespoons of the mushroom mixture along one short edge of each wrapper, roll up and set aside on the plastic wrap.

Preheat the oven to 400°F. For the béchamel sauce, bring the milk to a boil in a pan. Melt the butter in another pan, stir in the flour, and cook over low heat for 3–4 minutes, stirring, without letting it brown. Gradually stir in the hot milk and bring to a boil, stirring. Leave to simmer for 5 minutes, stirring frequently, until smooth and thick, then season to taste with salt and pepper.

Pour about one quarter of the sauce into a lightly buttered shallow baking dish just big enough to hold the *canalóns* in a single layer, and spread it over the base. Arrange the *canalóns* on top. Pour over the remaining sauce so that they are evenly covered and sprinkle with the grated cheese. Bake for 25–30 minutes, until richly golden brown and bubbling.

Bacalao, potato, and scallion tortilla

The most popular tortilla in Spain is one made with just potatoes. However, this one, flavored with salt cod and scallions, is pretty hard to beat. The trick to making a good tortilla is to add the cooked ingredients to the bowl of beaten eggs, not the other way around, to stir the mixture a little as soon as it is put into the pan until it just begins to thicken, then to cook it slowly until set almost all the way through. Flipping it over takes a bit of practice, but by using a large plate or pan lid you will soon get the hang of it. Don't be scared of making a tortilla. It is one of the easiest things in the world to master if you follow these few simple rules.

Serves 6

11 oz piece *bacalao* (salt cod)
1 lb potatoes
6 tablespoons extra-virgin olive oil
1 medium scallion, trimmed and thinly sliced
8 extra large free-range (cage-free) eggs
2–3 tablespoons chopped flat-leaf parsley
sea salt and freshly ground black pepper

Knock the excess salt off the *bacalao*, and place it, skin-side up, in a bowl. Cover with plenty of cold water and leave to soak for 24 hours, changing the water every 6 hours or so. After this time, take a small piece of fish from the thickest part and taste it. If it doesn't taste too salty, it's ready to use, but remember: salt cod needs to be a little bit salty, and also it will taste slightly more salty once it is cooked. Drain the pieces of salt cod, and put them into a pan with enough cold water to cover. Bring to a boil, remove from the heat, cover, and set aside for 10 minutes to cook gently in the heat of the water. Then lift out onto a plate, and when it is cool enough to handle, break the fish into flakes, discarding the skin and any bones. Cover and set aside.

Cut the potatoes into ½-inch-thick chunky matchsticks. Heat 4 tablespoons of the olive oil in a 9-inch nonstick frying pan, add the potatoes, and cook, stirring occasionally, for 15 minutes or until just tender, but not browned. You are not aiming for French fries here. Lift onto a plate with a slotted spoon, add the scallions to the pan, and cook for 2–3 minutes until just soft. Remove from the heat, and leave to cool slightly.

Beat the eggs in a mixing bowl with ½ teaspoon salt and some pepper. Stir in the fried potatoes, scallions, flaked *bacalao*, and chopped parsley. Wipe the frying pan clean. Reheat with another tablespoon of the olive oil over medium heat, and when it is hot, pour in the tortilla mixture, and cook, stirring it gently with a wooden spoon, for about 1 minute until thickened slightly. Smooth the mixture down, tidy up the edges, and leave to cook over gentle heat for 10 minutes, or until golden brown underneath and almost completely set.

Cover the pan with an upturned plate or large pan lid, turn them over together so that the tortilla is now on the lid, and return the pan to the heat, adding the remaining oil. Slide the tortilla back into the pan, and cook for another 2–3 minutes until just cooked through. Remove from the pan, and leave to cool slightly. Serve warm, cut into wedges.

Olive oil mash with poached eggs and truffle butter

The Spanish love eggs, but before I moved to England I rarely had the opportunity to eat poached eggs, because in Spain we usually serve them fried or boiled, scrambled, or set in tortillas. Poaching has become one of my favorite ways of eating them, and nothing is more pleasing than cutting into a perfectly soft yolk. People have questioned the combination of poached eggs and mashed potatoes because of the softness of both textures, but, I promise you, it works!

Serves 4

1 teaspoon white wine vinegar

4 very fresh extra large, free-range (cage-free) eggs

For the olive oil mashed potatoes

2 lb floury potatoes, such as Russet

4 garlic cloves, peeled, but left whole

1 bay leaf

4 tablespoons extra-virgin olive oil

½ cup whole milk

For the truffle butter

½ stick butter

1 black truffle

1 teaspoon truffle oil

sea salt and freshly ground black pepper

Cut the potatoes into large chunks. Put them into a pan of salted water with the garlic cloves and bay leaf. Bring to a boil and simmer for 15–20 minutes, or until the potatoes are tender. Meanwhile, bring 5 cups of water to a boil in a small pan. Drain the potatoes well, removing and discarding the garlic cloves and bay leaf, then press them through a potato ricer back into the pan. Beat in the olive oil, salt to taste, and enough of the milk to make a smooth, creamy mash. Cover, return it to low heat, and keep warm.

Reduce the heat under the small pan of water, so that the water is barely simmering, and add a large pinch of salt and the vinegar. Swirl it vigorously to ceate a whirlpool, and crack in one of the eggs. Leave it to poach for 3 minutes, then lift out with a slotted spoon onto a plate. Repeat with the rest of the eggs, keeping the water simmering.

For the truffle butter, melt the butter in a small pan. Peel the black, scaly outer layer from the truffle, and very finely grate it into the butter. Stir in the truffle oil, and some salt and pepper to taste. Keep hot.

Return the poached eggs to the simmering water and leave to heat through for 30 seconds, then lift out, and drain briefly on paper towels.

Spoon some of the hot olive oil mashed potato into 4 small warmed bowls, and place a poached egg on top. Spoon some of the truffle butter over each egg, sprinkle with a little sea salt, and serve.

Fresh and smoked salmon tartare

I love the mild, smoky flavor of the Spanish smoked salmon made by my friend Carlos Piernas. He is situated in the most beautiful national park in Catalonia where I spent an amazing week shooting photographs for this book. He marinates his salmon with sugar and salt, and then smokes it very lightly. When I go to see him I spend one lunch eating all the different cuts of salmon, from the less fatty tail to the most incredible taro (the piece below the belly). This is not his recipe, but I dedicate it to him for his hospitality. The salmon is left a little more raw and moist than other versions.

Serves 4

14 oz salmon fillet, skinned

3½ oz smoked salmon

2 tablespoons capers, rinsed, drained, and finely chopped

⅓ cup shallots, very finely chopped

2 tablespoons chopped flat-leaf parsley

6 cornichons (gherkins), finely chopped

8–10 dashes Tabasco sauce, according to taste

1 teaspoon sea salt flakes

2 tablespoons extra-virgin olive oil

2 teaspoons lemon juice

4 large egg yolks

freshly ground white pepper

fingers of toast, to serve

Thinly slice the salmon fillet and smoked salmon, then cut them into long thin strips about ¼ inch wide. Put them into a bowl with the capers, shallots, parsley, cornichons, Tabasco, sea salt, olive oil, lemon juice, and white pepper. Mix together well, spoon into the center of 4 chilled plates, and shape into a neat pile. Make a small hollow in the top of the mixture and add an egg yolk to each one. Serve with the fingers of toast.

Gambas à la gabardina with lemon

I can't tell you where to find the best *gambas a la gabardina* because there are so many delicious recipes from all over Spain, but I think the best one I ever tried was in Paramos. The shrimp cook inside the batter, keeping their succulence, so that when you bite into them you have a wonderful rich shrimp flavor.

Serves 4

1 lb (approx. 20) large raw unshelled shrimp

olive oil or sunflower oil, for deep-frying

2 large egg whites

fine sea salt

lemon wedges, to serve

For the batter

generous ¾ cup all-purpose flour

¼ teaspoon hot paprika

5 tablespoons olive oil

⅓ cup lager-style beer

⅓ cup cold water

Make the batter 30 minutes before you want to start cooking. Sift the flour, paprika, and a good pinch of salt into a mixing bowl. Make a well in the center, add the oil, lager, and water, and beat well together until you have a smooth batter. Cover and leave it to stand for 30 minutes.

Meanwhile, peel the shrimp, leaving the last tail segment in place. Shortly before cooking, heat some oil for deep-frying to 375°F. Whisk the egg whites in a bowl into soft peaks and gently fold into the batter.

Holding each shrimp by its tail, dip it into the batter, and add it to the hot oil. Cook 5–6 at a time for 2½–3 minutes, until crisp and golden. Drain briefly on paper towels while you cook the remainder, and serve hot with the lemon wedges.

Pan-fried sea bass with a salad of oranges, red onion, capers and black olives

The region of Valencia is famous for its citrus groves and particularly its oranges. There they regularly make a salad using flaked salt cod, oranges, onion and black olives, but I often like to substitute the salt cod with a freshly cooked fillet of fish; the fresh, summery flavors go so well together. This salad is also lovely made with blood oranges when they are in season.

Serves 4

8 x 3 oz sea bass fillets

1 tablespoon olive oil

sea salt and freshly ground black pepper

For the salad

4 small oranges

1 small red onion

4 teaspoons small capers, rinsed and drained

16 good-quality black olives, pitted and halved

For the vinaigrette

1 tablespoon freshly squeezed orange juice

1 tablespoon sherry vinegar

1½ tablespoons extra-virgin olive oil

1 heaping tablespoon chopped flat-leaf parsley

For the salad, cut a thin slice off the top and bottom of each orange and slice away all the skin, ensuring the white pith is completely removed. Then cut either side of each segment of fruit, close to the dividing membrane, down into the center of the orange, and drop the segments into a bowl.

Halve the onion and very thinly slice it, on a mandoline if possible, then separate the slices. Add them to the bowl of orange segments with the capers and black olives, and mix together gently.

For the vinaigrette, whisk the orange juice, sherry vinegar, and olive oil together in a small bowl and add some seasoning to taste. Stir in the chopped parsley.

Heat a large nonstick frying pan over medium heat. Rub the bream fillets with oil, and season on both sides. Add the fillets to the pan, skin-side down, and cook for 4–5 minutes until the skin is crisp and golden. Carefully turn the fillets over with a fish spatula, and cook for another 2 minutes, then remove the pan from the heat, and leave the fish to finish cooking in the heat of the pan.

Gently stir a heaping tablespoon of the vinaigrette into the salad, and adjust the seasoning to taste. Spoon some of the salad onto each plate, and rest the fish fillets on top. Drizzle a little more of the vinaigrette over the fish, and around the edge of the plate.

Rice with shrimp, pancetta, tomato, and peas

This simple rice dish, flavored with shrimp and pancetta, can be cooked in a shallow flameproof casserole, a terracotta *cazuela*, or large frying pan rather than a traditional paella pan, and makes an ideal supper dish for feeding a crowd.

Serves 6

½ teaspoon saffron (about 20 threads)
1 quart chicken stock
5 tablespoons extra-virgin olive oil
7 oz smoked pancetta, cut into short fat strips, or smoked bacon cubes
1 medium onion, finely chopped
4 garlic cloves, thinly sliced
12 oz skinned, chopped tomatoes, fresh or canned
1 teaspoon sweet paprika
2 cups paella rice (Calasparra or Bomba)
12 oz fresh or frozen peas
1 lb (18–20) large, raw unpeeled shrimp
sea salt and freshly ground black pepper

Shake the saffron strands around in a slightly hot frying pan for a few seconds until dry but not colored, then transfer into a small mortar or coffee cup, and grind to a powder with a pestle or a wooden spoon. Add a splash of the chicken stock, and set aside.

Heat 3 tablespoons of the olive oil in a 11–12-inch terracotta *cazuela*, or shallow flameproof casserole. Add the pancetta, and fry until it is crisp and golden, then stir in the onion and garlic, and fry gently for 8–10 minutes until soft and lightly golden. Stir in the tomatoes and paprika and fry for another 2–3 minutes, until the tomatoes start to soften. Stir in the saffron mixture, the rest of the stock and 1½ teaspoons salt, and bring to a boil. Sprinkle in the rice, stir once and leave to simmer a little vigorously for 6 minutes. Sprinkle over the peas, then reduce the heat, and leave to simmer more gently for 14 minutes until the rice is *al punto*, or still with a little bite to it.

Shortly before the rice is cooked, rub the shrimp with the remaining oil and season well with salt and pepper. Heat a large frying pan/flat cast-iron grill pan over high heat. Place the shrimp side by side in the pan, reduce the heat to medium, and cook for 2–2½ minutes on each side until just cooked through (they will continue to cook once they are on top of the rice). Arrange the shrimp on top of the rice, turn off the heat, cover the casserole with a kitchen towel or pan lid, and leave to rest for 5 minutes before serving.

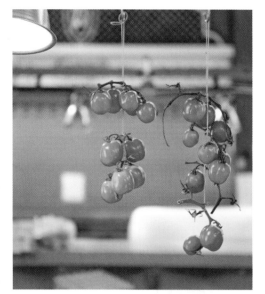

Sautéed squid with black rice and alioli

It's not always easy to find uncleaned squid, and preparing it yourself does involve a bit of work. The alternative is to buy ready-prepared squid from a fish market, together with a pack or two of squid ink, which will guarantee that you end up with enough ink to give the rice its characteristic black color.

Serves 6

1½ lb uncleaned squid (or buy ready-prepared with 1–2 packs of squid ink)

1 quart fish stock

7 tablespoons extra-virgin olive oil

2 medium onions, finely chopped

2 large garlic cloves, finely chopped

7 oz skinned, chopped tomatoes, fresh or canned

²/₃ cup dry white wine

2 cups paella rice (Calasparra or Bomba)

sea salt and freshly ground black pepper

1 quantity Alioli (see page 227), to serve

If you are using uncleaned squid, you need to remove and save the ink sacs from inside the pouches. Pull the heads away from the pouches, taking with them the intestines and clear quill. Locate the ink sacs (they resemble pearly blue-white sacs), detach them, and set them aside. Cut the tentacles away from the heads, just in front of the eyes, and discard the rest. Pull the fins away from the bodies, and pull away the grey membranous skin from both. Rinse out the squid pouches with cold water, then slice them and the fins crosswise into ¼-inch-wide strips. Separate the tentacles into pairs. To extract the ink from the sacs, put some of the fish stock into a bowl and, one at a time, slit open the sacs and rinse them out in the stock. Discard the sacs.

Heat 3 tablespoons of the oil in a 18-inch paella pan. Add the onions and garlic, and fry gently for 6–8 minutes until soft and lightly golden. Add the tomatoes, and cook for 4–5 minutes until softened, then stir in the wine, and simmer for another 3–4 minutes until it has almost disappeared. Stir in the inky fish stock and remaining stock, and bring to a boil. Scatter over the rice, stir once so that it is evenly distributed around the pan, and leave to simmer quite vigorously for 6 minutes. Reduce the heat, and leave to simmer gently for another 14 minutes, until all the stock has been absorbed and the rice is pitted with small holes. Turn off the heat, cover with a clean kitchen towel, or a large pan lid, and leave to rest for 5 minutes.

Meanwhile, heat another 2 tablespoons of oil in a large frying pan. Add half the squid, and stir-fry over high heat for 2 minutes, seasoning it as it cooks, until nicely browned and just cooked through. Transfer to a plate, and repeat with the remainder. Uncover the rice, scatter over the squid, and serve with the alioli.

Pasta with chorizo and mussels

Pasta is popular in the east of Spain. You might wonder why a Spanish chef is cooking with pasta, but so many Italian chefs are cooking wonderful dishes with chorizo, so why not? I created this dish with my friend Diego in Barcelona. I still remember buying the mussels from La Boqueria, the famous food market in that city, and marrying the flavors with a very nice glass of red wine from Priorat.

Serves 4

6 tablespoons extra-virgin olive oil

3 garlic cloves, finely chopped

½ teaspoon crushed dried red pepper flakes

14 oz skinned, chopped tomatoes, fresh or canned

2¼ lb fresh mussels

14 oz dried spaghetti

6 tablespoons dry white wine

7 oz cooking chorizo sausage, skinned and diced

2 tablespoons chopped flat-leaf parsley

sea salt and freshly ground black pepper

Put 4 tablespoons of the olive oil, the garlic and dried red pepper flakes in a large frying pan or saucepan and place it over medium-high heat. As soon as the garlic is sizzling, add the tomatoes, and simmer gently for 15 minutes until well reduced, quite thick, and just starting to stick to the bottom of the pan.

Meanwhile, bring a large pan of salted water to a boil. Wash the mussels, pull out the beards from between the tightly closed shells, and discard any that are open, and won't close when tapped on a work surface. Add the spaghetti to the boiling water, and cook for 10–11 minutes, or until *al punto*—still with a little bite.

Heat another large pan over high heat, add the mussels and the wine, cover, and cook for 2–3 minutes, shaking the pan occasionally, until all the mussels are only just open. Take care not to overcook them at this stage. Pour them into a colander placed over a bowl to collect the cooking juices. Stir all but the last tablespoon or two of the cooking liquid into the tomato sauce, and continue to simmer until the sauce has reduced and thickened once more, but is a little more moist than before. Season to taste with salt and pepper. Remove half of the larger mussels from their shells.

Heat the remaining olive oil in a frying pan, add the chorizo and fry gently for 1 minute until lightly golden. Drain the spaghetti, return to the pan, and add the tomato sauce, cooked mussels, chorizo sausage, and chopped parsley. Toss well together and serve.

Grilled sausages with arrocina beans, garlic, and sage

For this dish it is really important to get meaty continental-style fresh sausages. Those from Spain called *butifarra blanca*, or from southern France such as Toulouse, or Italy's *salsicche*, are 100 per cent pure meat, flavored with spices, without any filler. The arrocina beans are small, sweet and meaty dried beans. If you can't get hold of them, use dried haricot or cannellini beans.

Serves 4

11 oz dried small white beans, such as arrocina, soaked overnight in cold water

1 medium onion, halved

4 cloves

4 bay leaves

1 head of garlic, halved, plus 3 garlic cloves, finely chopped

4–8 large fresh meaty pork sausages (*butifarra* if possible)

4 tablespoons extra-virgin olive oil

12 large sage leaves, finely chopped

12 oz vine-ripened tomatoes

sea salt and freshly ground black pepper

Drain the beans, put them into a pan with 1 quart cold water, and bring them to a boil. Meanwhile, stud the onion halves with the cloves. Skim the scum from the surface of the beans, add the onion halves, bay leaves and garlic bulb, reduce the heat, cover, and leave to simmer gently for 1–1½ hours, or until the beans are tender, adding 1 teaspoon salt 5 minutes before the end of the cooking time. Drain, remove and discard the onion, bay leaves, and garlic, and set aside.

Heat a ridged or flat cast-iron griddle, or a heavy-based frying pan over high heat. Rub the sausages with a little of the oil, add them to the griddle or pan, reduce the heat to medium, and cook for 8–10 minutes, turning them now and then, until they are golden brown and cooked through.

Meanwhile, skin the tomatoes, quarter them and scoop the seeds into a sieve set over a bowl. Rub through the juices with a wooden spoon, and cut the flesh into small pieces.

Shortly before the sausages are ready, heat the remaining olive oil and the chopped garlic in a large frying pan over medium heat. As soon as the garlic is sizzling, add the sage and leave it to cook for a few seconds. Add the beans, and stir gently for 3–4 minutes, until they have heated through. Stir in the tomatoes and their juices and cook gently for a further 2–3 minutes, so that the pieces of tomato retain their shape. Season generously to taste (beans need plenty of seasoning) with salt and pepper, and serve with the grilled sausages.

Caldoso with quail, wild mushrooms, artichokes, and black olives

Spain has many great rice dishes, paella being the most famous. *Caldoso*, a soupy rice dish, follows the same cooking principles but just uses double the amount of stock, so it is more like a rice casserole than a paella. This is a surprisingly easy dish to make, and extremely comforting and tasty to eat. Do try it for a change the next time you think about making a paella. If quail are a bit tricky to find, use skinned chicken thighs instead—it will still taste delicious.

Serves 4

1 cup dried wild mushrooms, such as porcini

4 oven-ready quail

2 tablespoons extra-virgin olive oil

1 cooking chorizo sausage (approx 4 oz), skinned and cut into small dice

1 medium onion, chopped

2 large garlic cloves, finely chopped

12 oz small ceps, sliced, or button chestnut mushrooms, halved if large

leaves from 2 large thyme sprigs

leaves from a 6-inch rosemary sprig, chopped

½ teaspoon sweet paprika

9 oz vine-ripened tomatoes, skinned and chopped

5 cups chicken stock

1½ cups paella rice (preferably Calasparra)

4 fresh bay leaves

10 oz jar artichoke hearts or bottoms in olive oil, drained and halved if large

½ cup black olives, pitted

sea salt and freshly ground black pepper

2 tablespoons chopped flat-leaf parsley, to garnish

Put the dried mushrooms into a small bowl, and cover with boiling water. Leave to soak for 30 minutes. Meanwhile, cut along either side of the backbone of each quail with kitchen scissors, remove it and discard. Open out each quail flat and cut in half along the breastbone, then into quarters by cutting the legs away from the breasts. Remove the small rib bones from the underside of each breast, and season all the pieces well with salt and pepper.

Heat the oil in a large flameproof casserole or pan. Add half the quail pieces skin-side down, and fry for 3–4 minutes until golden brown. Turn over, and fry for 2 minutes more, then transfer from the pan to a plate. Repeat with the remaining quail pieces.

Add the chorizo to the casserole, and fry for 1 minute until lightly golden. Add the onion and garlic, and fry for 5–6 minutes over medium heat until soft and lightly golden. Drain the rehydrated mushrooms and squeeze them dry. Add them to the onions and garlic with the fresh mushrooms, thyme, rosemary, and a little more seasoning and fry, stirring, for another 4 minutes. Stir in the paprika, fry for 30 seconds, then add the tomatoes and cook for 2 minutes until softened.

Return the quail pieces to the pan with the stock, and bring to a boil. Stir in the rice and bay leaves, and season to taste with salt and pepper. Reduce the heat, and leave to simmer for 18 minutes, stirring occasionally, until the rice is almost cooked.

When the rice is nearly done, stir in the artichokes and black olives, and simmer for 2 minutes, stirring. Serve in large warmed soup plates, scattered with the chopped parsley.

Roast chicken with cava and apples

In Spain, roast chicken is not traditionally served with a slightly thickened gravy as in the UK, but after living here for 10 years or more I like to do some things the British way. However, I take a tip from my mother and combine chicken with apples. Why not? It's delicious, especially if you serve it with some more cava!

Serves 4–6

1 x 3¼ lb free-range (cage-free) chicken

4 fresh bay leaves

2 large thyme sprigs

olive oil, for greasing the bird

2 medium onions, cut into thin wedges

6 garlic cloves, thinly sliced

1 bottle cava (Spanish sparkling wine)

4 small dessert apples, such as Mcintosh

2 tablespoons butter

2 teaspoons superfine sugar

¼ teaspoon ground cinnamon

scant ½ cup chicken stock

1 teaspoon soft butter

1 teaspoon plain flour

sea salt and freshly ground black pepper

Preheat the oven to 400°F. Season the cavity of the chicken with salt and pepper, and then stuff with the bay leaves and thyme. Tie the legs together with string, then rub all over with olive oil, and season well with salt and pepper. Place in the center of a large roasting pan, and roast for 30 minutes.

Remove the roasting pan from the oven, and scatter the onions and garlic around the chicken. Stir them into the cooking juices, season lightly, pour 3 tablespoons of the cava over the bird and return it to the oven for 45 minutes, basting it every 10 minutes with a another 3 tablespoons of the cava.

While the chicken is roasting, quarter, core, and peel the apples, and cut them into small wedges. Melt the butter in a frying pan, add the apples, and fry them for 2 minutes until they begin to brown. Turn the slices over, sprinkle with the sugar and cinnamon, and continue to fry for another 2 minutes, until they are just tender and nicely golden. Remove from the heat.

When the chicken is cooked and the juices run clear, lift it onto a board, wrap it in foil and leave it to rest for 10 minutes. Scoop the onions out of the roasting juices, add them to the apples, and mix well together. Season lightly to taste, and keep warm over low heat.

Tip the roasting pan so that the remaining pan juices pool at one end, and skim off the excess fat. Then place the pan over medium-high heat, add another ½ cup of the cava and the stock, and scrape the base of the pan with a wooden spoon to release all the caramelized juices. Strain into a small pan, and simmer for about 10 minutes until reduced and well-flavored. Mix the soft butter with the plain flour, whisk it into the gravy, and simmer gently for 2–3 minutes. Season to taste with salt and pepper.

Carve the chicken. Spoon some the onions and apples onto each warmed plate, and put the chicken on top. Pour over the gravy and serve.

Braised chicken with tomatoes, salsify, and almonds

There was a time when the only chickens you could buy in Spain were those that were truly free-range with very little meat covering the breast and dark, almost gamey-tasting meat. Today Spanish chickens are more similar to the birds reared in the US and braised chicken is second only to *pollo al ajillo* (chicken fried with garlic) in popularity. If you can't get salsify, use young slender parsnips, cut lengthwise into quarters—the dish will taste just as good.

Serves 6

2¼ lb salsify (scorzonera)

juice of 1 lemon

6 tablespoons extra-virgin olive oil

4 garlic cloves, peeled

¼ cup blanched almonds, toasted

3 tablespoons flat-leaf parsley, plus extra, chopped, to garnish

2 cups chicken stock

1 x 4 lb chicken, cut into 8–10 pieces

4 oz pancetta or bacon cubes

1 large onion, finely chopped

14 oz skinned, chopped tomatoes, fresh or canned

1 teaspoon superfine sugar

heaping ¼ cup flour

sea salt and freshly ground black pepper

Peel the salsify and cut each piece lengthwise into thirds, dropping them immediately into a bowl of cold water, acidulated with the lemon juice, to prevent them from turning brown. Bring a large pan of salted water to a boil. Add the salsify and simmer for 15–20 minutes, or until just tender. Drain well, then leave to dry on a clean kitchen towel, or paper towels.

Heat 2 tablespoons of the olive oil in a shallow flameproof casserole, or large deep frying pan. Add the garlic cloves and fry them gently for 2–3 minutes until soft and golden brown. Put them into a mini food processor with the toasted almonds, parsley leaves, and 3–4 tablespoons of the stock. Blend to a smooth paste, then set aside.

Add another 2 tablespoons of the olive oil to the pan and place over medium-high heat. Add half of the chicken pieces, season them with salt and pepper, and fry for about 8–10 minutes, until deep golden brown all over. Lift onto a plate and repeat with the rest of the chicken.

Add the pancetta or bacon to the pan, and fry until crisp and golden. Lift out with a slotted spoon and set aside with the chicken. Add the onion to the pan, and fry gently for 8–10 minutes until golden brown. Add the tomatoes and sugar, reduce the heat slightly, and simmer for 5 minutes until the tomatoes have broken down, and thickened into a sauce.

Meanwhile, heat the remaining oil in another nonstick frying pan over medium-high heat. Working in batches, season the salsify, then dust in the flour, and fry, turning occasionally, until crisp and golden brown all over. Transfer each batch to a tray lined with paper towels.

Stir the remaining stock into the tomato sauce, add the fried chicken and pancetta or bacon, cover and simmer for 20 minutes. Stir in the salsify and simmer, uncovered, for another 15 minutes, until the chicken is tender and the sauce has reduced and thickened. Stir in the almond and garlic paste, and some seasoning to taste, and simmer for another 5 minutes. Serve garnished with chopped parsley.

Duck with orange, Spanish style

I love the classic combination of duck with oranges, but this dish is a little different with the addition of cinnamon and honey. The total cooking time I allow for a roast duck is 15 minutes per pound, which results in a very slightly pink and juicy meat. I use Valencian oranges because they are the best, obviously!

Serves 4

1 x 4½ lb oven-ready duck

fine sea salt and freshly ground black pepper

watercress, to garnish

For the orange sauce

4–5 oranges

2 tablespoons superfine sugar

4 tablespoons red wine vinegar

2 cups chicken or duck stock

2 teaspoons honey

2-inch cinnamon stick

1 tablespoon lemon juice

1 teaspoon arrowroot

If you have time, unwrap the duck, dry it well inside and out with paper towels and leave it somewhere cool for the skin to dry off, overnight if possible.

Preheat the oven to 450°F. Season the cavity of the duck with salt and pepper, and the skin just with salt. Place it on a rack in a large roasting pan, and roast for 20 minutes. Then remove it from the oven, and pour the excess fat from the pan into a small bowl. Reduce the oven temperature to 350°F, return the duck, and continue to roast for 40 minutes, pouring the fat from the pan into a small bowl every 15–20 minutes. (Don't discard it: duck fat is excellent for roast potatoes.)

Meanwhile, for the sauce, peel the zest from half of 1 orange and cut it into long, fine shreds. Drop them into a pan of boiling water, leave for 5 seconds, then drain and refresh under cold water. Set aside to drain on paper towels. Next, cut a thin slice off the top and bottom of 2 of the oranges and slice away all the skin, ensuring the white pith is completely removed. Then cut either side of each segment of fruit, close to the dividing membrane, down into the center of the orange, and drop the segments into a bowl. Set aside. Squeeze the juice from the remaining oranges and measure out 5 fl oz of juice.

Put the sugar and vinegar into a small pan, and leave over low heat until the sugar has dissolved. Increase the heat and boil rapidly until it has turned into a dark, amber-colored caramel. Remove from the heat and carefully add the stock (take care as it will splutter quite a bit), the honey, orange juice, and cinnamon stick. Bring to a boil, and simmer rapidly until reduced by three-quarters to 5 fl oz. Remove the cinnamon stick, stir in the lemon juice and a little seasoning to taste, and bring back to a simmer. Mix the arrowroot with 1 tablespoon water, stir into the sauce, and simmer for 1 minute, until thickened and clear. Stir in the shredded orange zest and keep warm.

Remove the duck from the oven, lift it onto a board, cover loosely with foil and leave to rest for 5–10 minutes. Add the orange segments to the sauce, and bring it back to a simmer. Carve the legs off the duck and cut each one in half at the joint. Cut each of the breasts away from the carcass in one piece and cut each one lengthwise into long thin slices. Arrange the meat on warmed plates, spoon over the sauce and serve, garnished with the watercress.

Cava and lemon sorbet with candied lemon peel

There is nothing better than to finish a meal with a cleansing sorbet. In Spain, people often use a lemon sorbet between courses to cleanse the palate. I never understand that as I think the best way to clean the palate is a nice glass of wine! This sorbet is best served soon after churning and freezing, and doesn't improve on keeping. The candied lemon peel adds that necessary sweetness.

Serves 10–12

4 large juicy lemons

1¾ cups superfine sugar

5 tablespoons liquid glucose, plus
  1 tablespoon

pinch of salt

1 x 25 fl oz bottle of cava

For the candied lemon peel, pare wide strips of peel from the lemons using a sharp vegetable peeler, ensuring none of the bitter white pith is included. Cut the parings lengthwise into $1/8$-inch-wide strips. Put them into a pan with enough cold water to cover, bring to a boil, and simmer for 15 minutes, then drain and refresh under cold water.

Put 1 cup of the sugar, 1 tablespoon of the liquid glucose, a pinch of salt and 2 cups water into a clean pan. Bring to a boil, add the blanched lemon peel, and leave to simmer until the mixtures registers 225°F on a sugar thermometer. Remove from the heat, lift the strands of peel out of the syrup with a fork, and curl them attractively on a large baking sheet lined with parchment paper. Leave to go cold, then finely chop about half of them and set aside. Reserve some of the prettiest strands for decoration, and store the remainder in an airtight container for a future batch of sorbet.

For the sorbet, pour half the cava into a pan, and add the remaining sugar and liquid glucose. Bring slowly to a boil, stirring to dissolve the sugar, then remove from the heat and leave to cool. Meanwhile, squeeze the pared lemons to yield about 1 scant cup of juice. Stir the remaining cava into the cooled syrup with the lemon juice, strain the mixture into a bowl, cover and leave to chill overnight.

The next day, churn the sorbet mixture in an ice cream machine. Alternatively, pour it into a shallow container and freeze until almost solid. Scrape into the bowl of a food processor and blend briefly until smooth, then return to the container and freeze once more. Repeat this 2–3 times more, until the mixture is very smooth. Stir in the chopped candied lemon peel towards the end of churning, or after blending for the final time. Spoon back into the container, and freeze for at least 6 hours or until firm. Serve in scoops, decorated with the reserved pieces of candied peel.

Roasted hazelnut ice cream

Reus, in the province of Tarragona, is the center of hazelnut production in Spain, but today the industry is seriously threatened by competition from Turkey. In an effort to help the Spanish industry and halt the trend for using cheaper imported hazelnuts, the EU awarded the nuts from this region a mark of quality called the Denominación de Origen. Today they are highly revered and go into the production of many confectionery and nut pastries of the region. This is one of my favorite ice creams.

Serves 6–8

For the hazelnut paste

8 oz shelled hazelnuts

1 large egg white

heaping ⅓ cup confectioners' sugar, sifted

2 tablespoons hazelnut liqueur (optional)

For the ice cream

1 vanilla bean

1 scant cup whole milk

3 extra large egg yolks

½ cup superfine sugar

1¼ cups heavy cream

For the hazelnut paste, preheat the oven to 400°F. Spread the nuts on a baking sheet and roast for 12–15 minutes or until richly golden. Remove and leave to cool, then rub off the skins in a clean kitchen towel. Drop half the nuts into a food processor and grind very finely. Pour into a bowl and grind the remaining nuts. Return the first batch to the food processor with the egg white, sugar and hazelnut liqueur, if using, and blend to a smooth paste.

For the ice cream, slit open the vanilla bean and scrape out all the seeds. Put the bean and seeds into a pan with the milk, and slowly bring to a boil. Gently whisk the egg yolks and sugar together in a bowl until pale and creamy. Remove the vanilla bean from the milk, and gradually whisk the hot milk into the egg yolks. Return the mixture to a clean pan, and cook over low heat, stirring, until the mixture lightly coats the back of a wooden spoon. Leave to cool, then strain into the food processor and blend with the hazelnut paste. Transfer to a bowl, cover, and chill overnight.

The next day, stir the cream into the hazelnut custard, and churn the ice cream mixture in an ice cream machine. Alternatively, pour it into a shallow container and freeze until almost solid. Scrape into the bowl of a food processor, and blend briefly until smooth, then return to the container, and freeze once more. Repeat this 2–3 times more, until the mixture is very smooth, then return to the freezer for 6 hours or until firm and ready to use.

Apricots in cava

This is a really simple and quick dessert. It celebrates the very best of ripe summer fruits—just make sure your apricots are ripe and sweet.

Serves 6–8

12 ripe apricots

3 tablespoons superfine sugar, or to taste

4 tablespoons peach liqueur

7 oz fresh raspberries

2 cups chilled cava or sparkling rosé wine

Peel the apricots, then halve the fruit, remove the pits, and slice the fruit into a glass serving bowl. Sprinkle over the sugar and peach liqueur, and toss together gently. Cover and chill until needed.

Shortly before serving, sprinkle the raspberries over a plate and lightly crush them with the back of a fork. Stir them into the apricots, pour over the sparkling wine and serve immediately.

Blood orange sorbet

It wasn't until I came to Britain thirteen years ago that I saw a blood orange. And now I wait all year for them to come back into season—I love them that much! This sorbet is simple to make and one of the nicest ways in which to enjoy their sweet sharp flavor and beautiful deep red color.

Serves 6–8

½ cup superfine sugar

¼ cup liquid glucose

½ cup water

12 blood oranges

juice of 1 lemon

Put the sugar, liquid glucose, and water into a pan, and bring slowly to a boil, stirring occasionally to dissolve the sugar. Remove from the heat, and leave to cool.

Squeeze the blood oranges to yield about 2½ cups of juice. Stir it into the cooled syrup with the lemon juice, strain into a bowl and chill overnight.

The next day, churn the sorbet mixture in an ice cream machine. Alternatively, pour it into a shallow container, and freeze until almost solid. Scrape into the bowl of a food processor. and blend briefly until smooth, then return to the container, and freeze once more. Repeat this 2–3 times more, until the mixture is very smooth. Spoon back into the container, and freeze for at least 6 hours or until firm. This is lovely served in scoops with a mixture of orange and blood orange wedges, dressed with a little sugar and lemon juice.

Almond bizcocho with caramel oranges

A *bizcocho* is a simple loaf-shaped cake, which is regularly served for afternoon tea in Spain. My sister Isabel always makes one when I visit her. I love to eat *bizcocho* while it is still slightly warm from the oven. However, it also makes an excellent dessert, especially if served with caramel oranges, so that the delicious juices soak into the sponge. A scoop of ice cream on the side is pretty good too. If you can't get blood oranges—sadly they are around only for a few short weeks during the winter months —use small juicy normal oranges instead.

Serves 8

7 fl oz mild olive oil, plus extra for greasing

1⅓ cups all-purpose flour

2 teaspoons baking powder

pinch of salt

1 cup ground almonds

generous ¾ cup superfine sugar

3 extra large, free-range (cage-free) eggs, lightly beaten

finely grated zest of 1 orange

7 tablespoons freshly squeezed orange juice

For the caramel oranges

8 blood oranges or small, juicy oranges

1 cup superfine sugar

6 tablespoons freshly squeezed orange juice, strained

For the caramel oranges, cut a slice off the top and bottom of each orange, then slice away all the skin, ensuring the white pith is completely removed. Cut each orange across the segments into slices, reserving all the juices. Put the sugar into a large pan with ½ cup cold water. Leave over low heat until the sugar has dissolved, then bring to a boil, and boil rapidly until the syrup has turned into a brick-red caramel. Remove from the heat, and plunge the base of the pan into cold water, to stop it cooking any further. Stand back (as it will splutter slightly) and add the orange juice. The caramel will form a lump in the bottom of the pan. Return it to low heat, and stir until it dissolves again. Leave to cool very slightly, then, while it is still liquid, pour over the sliced oranges and chill for at least 1 hour.

For the almond *bizcocho*, preheat the oven to 325°F. Grease a 9 x 5 x 3-inch loaf pan with olive oil and line with parchment paper. Sift the flour, baking powder, and salt into a mixing bowl and stir in the ground almonds and superfine sugar. Make a well in the center, and add the beaten eggs, olive oil, orange zest, and juice. Gradually mix the dry ingredients into the wet to make a smooth batter.

Pour the mixture into the prepared pan, and bake for about 1 hour, covering the surface loosely with a sheet of paper after about 50 minutes, once it is a rich golden brown. A wooden toothpick, pushed into the center of the cake, should come away clean. Remove the cake from the pan, and peel back the lining paper. Leave to cool on a wire rack.

To serve, cut the cake into 16 slices. Place a slice onto each plate and spoon some of the caramel oranges partly over the slice. Top with another slice, and drizzle over a little more caramel syrup.

Chocolate and hazelnut tart

This is one of the best tarts I have ever eaten, and is a must for all chocolate and nut lovers. Once I start to eat it, I cannot stop. Try to serve it shortly after it comes out of the oven—still slightly puffed up and warm—but you can serve it cold if you like, and even a few days later. This is lovely served warm with cream or ice cream, but is just as good cold with a cup of coffee.

Serves 10–12

For the filling

2 heaping cups shelled hazelnuts

¾ cup good-quality dark chocolate, broken up (at least 70% cocoa solids)

¾ stick soft butter

¾ cup superfine sugar

finely grated zest of 1 orange

2 large eggs

1 tablespoon flour

3 tablespoons sweet sherry, such as Oloroso

For the pastry

1¾ cups all-purpose flour, plus extra for dusting

pinch of salt

½ cup confectioners' sugar

1 stick chilled butter, cut into small pieces

1 large egg yolk

5 teaspoons sweet sherry, such as Oloroso

For the pastry, sift the flour, salt, and confectioners' sugar into a food processor. Add the butter and process briefly until the mixture resembles fine breadcrumbs. Mix the egg yolk with the sherry. Pout the crumbed mixture into a bowl, stir in the egg yolk and sherry mixture, and bring the dough together into a ball. Turn out onto a lightly floured surface, and knead briefly until smooth. Shape into a flat disc, wrap in plastic wrap and chill for 15 minutes.

Remove the pastry from the fridge and roll it out thinly on a lightly floured surface. Use to line a 10 x 1½-inch deep loose-based tart pan. Refrigerate again for 20 minutes.

Put a baking sheet on the middle shelf of the oven and preheat it to 400°F. Line the pastry case with foil and a thin layer of baking beans, and bake for 15 minutes. Remove the foil and beans, and bake for another 4–5 minutes until crisp and golden brown. Remove and set aside. Spread the hazelnuts onto a baking sheet and roast for about 8 minutes until richly golden. Remove and allow to cool. Reduce the oven temperature to 325°F.

For the filling, grind the hazelnuts finely in a food processor until they resemble coarse breadcrumbs, but leave some of them a little chunky. Put the chocolate into a small heatproof bowl set over a pan of barely simmering water. Take the pan off the heat and leave until the chocolate has melted, then lift the bowl off the pan, and allow the chocolate to cool. Beat the butter, sugar, and orange zest together in a bowl until light and fluffy. Beat in the eggs, one at a time, adding a little of the flour with the second egg to stop the mixture from curdling. Fold in the remaining flour, the ground hazelnuts, melted chocolate, and lastly, the sherry. Spoon the mixture into the pastry case and bake for 30 minutes, by which time it should be slightly risen, and feel firm to the touch in the center. Remove and leave to cool slightly before serving, and dust with confectioners' sugar, if desired.

THE CENTER

THE CENTER: INTRODUCTION

Central Spain is the home of the conquistadors and Don Quixote, and includes my beloved Extremadura, which is where my family are from. My favorite time to visit is during autumn, when the saffron is being picked, peppers are being smoked to make pimentón (paprika) and hunting becomes a national pastime.

Madrid is where I learned about *nueva cocina*, working for my dear friend and mentor Julio Reoyo, whose restaurant is Mesón de Doña Filo. In the sixteeenth century, people from all over Spain flocked to Madrid, so not only is it a melting pot, but it boasts many restaurants that specialize in dishes from every region. Should you be wondering why this chapter contains recipes using sea fish even though the area is landlocked, believe it or not, Madrid has the best fish market in Spain. And no visit to the capital should exclude a trip to the San Miguel market for tapas, or to one of the bars that surround it for a nice cold beer and a sandwich filled with deep-fried calamari (squid)… heaven on earth and the best cure for a hangover!

Extremadura used to be a bit off the beaten track for tourists, but its popularity is growing and, obviously being my home, I can see why! There are so many places in the region that you must see. Guadelupe is the town where Christopher Columbus came (first to gain sponsorship from King Ferdinand and Queen Isabella, and the blessing of a safe voyage from the Virgin Mary of Guadalupe, and second, on his successful return from the New World, to show thanks), carrying with him highly significant ingredients that we now automatically associate with Spain—peppers, tomatoes and potatoes. These were grown by the monks of Guadalupe, and they were the first to make pimentón by smoking and grinding the peppers into a powder. Pimentón gives chorizo its distinctive color and intense flavor. Restaurants and bars in the city of Trujilo serve the local dish of *mijas*—breadcrumbs fried with olive oil and garlic and served with chorizo, fried peppers, and pancetta. Extremadura also produces *jamón Ibérico*, one of the finest of Spain's air-cured hams, and indeed all the products from the Ibérico pig—pork loin, morcilla, chorizo, and the fresh meat. If you come to my bar or restaurant in London, you must try some of the different cuts of Ibérico, like *pluma*, the fillet, and the cheeks.

The arid, high plateau of Castile-La Mancha is particularly famous because of the fictional knight Don Quixote, but in culinary terms it is the source of Manchego cheese, and, in my opinion, the best saffron in the world. The game from this area is exceptional— I particularly love the partridge. As in all of Spain, it is the simple, traditional fare eaten by the locals for centuries that marry the regional ingredients so perfectly. A rustic dish of beans, partridge, and local herbs can be one of the tastiest meals you will ever have.

Further north, Castile and León is the heart of legume-growing in Spain, in particular *garbanzos* (chickpeas), Pardina lentils and the *Judías* (white beans), which are used in regional everyday dishes. Morcilla de Burgos, a type of blood sausage containing rice, is a gourmet delight. My favorite way of serving this morcilla is pan-fried, topped with a fried egg.

Aragón is a land of hard winters and very warm summers. I have included Aragón in this chapter because its key ingredients and style of cooking are similar to the rural areas in the Center. Lamb and game from the Pyrenees are integral to the local cusine, but to me, the most important of all products from this region is the *jamón de Teruel*, which has great aroma and flavor. The differences between this and the equally top-quality *jamón Ibérico* are the breed of pig, the feed, and the curing process, so don't ever think these hams are the same!

If you are visiting any of these central regions, you must try the lamb. There is almost nothing better than a slow-roasted shoulder with some white wine, olive oil, thyme and garlic…

Chickpea soup with seared shrimp, chorizo, and paprika oil

Chickpeas and chorizo are a common combination in Spain, but making a soup with these flavors is unusual. My tip is to add some shrimp to give a little sweetness. Altogether, it is a very satisfying, winter warming dish.

Serves 4

8 tablespoons extra-virgin olive oil

2 medium onions, chopped

½ teaspoon crushed dried red pepper flakes

11 oz dried chickpeas (garbanzo beans), soaked for 24–48 hours in cold water

1 bay leaf

2 fat garlic cloves, thinly sliced

¾ teaspoon sweet paprika

1 teaspoon freshly ground coriander seeds

juice of ½ lemon

12 large raw peeled shrimp

4 oz cooking chorizo sausage, skinned and thinly sliced

sea salt and freshly ground black pepper

Heat 6 tablespoons of the oil in a large saucepan. Add the onions and red pepper flakes, cover, and fry gently for 10 minutes, until the onions are very soft and lightly golden. Scoop half the onions into another pan and set aside. Drain the chickpeas, and add them to the first pan with the bay leaf and 1 quart cold water. Bring to a boil, cover, and simmer gently for 2–2½ hours or until the chickpeas are very tender. Remove and discard the bay leaf.

Shortly before the chickpeas are ready, place the second pan of fried onions over medium heat. As soon as they are sizzling, stir in the garlic, ½ teaspoon of the paprika and the ground coriander, and fry gently for 2–3 minutes. Stir in the chickpeas and their cooking liquor and leave to cool slightly. Then blend, in batches if necessary, until very smooth. Return to the pan and stir in about 1 cup more water, or enough to give the soup a good consistency. Stir in the lemon juice, season to taste with salt and pepper, and bring back to a gentle simmer over low heat.

Heat the remaining oil in a frying pan over medium heat. Add the shrimp and sliced chorizo sausage, and fry for 2 minutes until the shrimps are just cooked through. Ladle the soup into warmed bowls and garnish with the fried shrimp and chorizo. Add the remaining paprika to the frying pan, and leave to sizzle gently for a few seconds. Drizzle the oil over the soup and serve.

Melon, cherry tomato, cucumber, and mint salad with Serrano ham

I think the saltiness of the ham and the sweetness of the melon work beautifully together. I love to add some crisp cucumber and ripe tomatoes to the melon as well, with finely shredded mint. Serve with crusty bread for an ideal summertime lunch or appetizer. This combination of ingredients is popular in all Mediterranean countries, but of course I use Serrano ham and Spanish tomatoes. And you can make the ham crispy by frying in some olive oil to give more texture to the dish.

Serves 4

½ charentais or canteloupe melon

½ cucumber

6 oz vine-ripened cherry tomatoes, halved

1 tablespoon finely shredded fresh mint

12 thin slices Serrano ham

For the vinaigrette

2 teaspoons red wine vinegar

½ teaspoon honey

1½ tablespoons extra-virgin olive oil

sea salt and freshly ground black pepper

Divide the melon into four wedges; scoop out and discard the seeds. Slice the flesh away from the skin and cut it into small pieces, about the same size as the halved cherry tomatoes. Peel the cucumber, quarter it lengthwise and cut into similar-sized pieces. Put the melon, tomatoes and cucumber in a serving bowl with the shredded mint, and toss together gently until the mint is well distributed.

Make the vinaigrette by whisking the vinegar, honey, and oil together with some salt and black pepper to taste. Stir into the salad. Arrange the Serrano ham slices on 4 plates and serve with the salad and fresh bread.

Braised peas and ham with eggs

This dish was one of my favorites when I was a student. It is really easy to make and filling—perfect for your pocket. These braised peas (without the egg) would make a lovely side dish, maybe with a piece of simply grilled chicken or fish. You can bake this recipe in individual small dishes as well—easy for a simple supper for one after work. Add some chopped mint if you have some, to give freshness to the dish.

Serves 2

2 extra-large, free-range (cage-free) eggs

sea salt and freshly ground black pepper

For the braised peas

3 tablespoons olive oil

¾ cup shallots, finely chopped

4 garlic cloves, thinly sliced

1 lb shelled peas, fresh or frozen

½ cup homemade chicken stock

3 oz thinly sliced Serrano ham, finely shredded

Heat the olive oil in a medium frying pan. Add the shallots and garlic, cover, and cook gently for 5 minutes until soft, but not browned. Stir in the peas and chicken stock, partially cover, and simmer gently for 5 minutes until the peas are tender, and the liquid has reduced to leave them just moist. Stir in the Serrano ham, and season to taste with salt and pepper.

Break the eggs, spaced well apart, on top of the peas, season lightly and cover the pan with a tightly-fitting lid. Leave to cook gently for 5 minutes, or until the eggs are set to your liking. Eat with some crusty fresh bread.

Pardina lentils with soft goat cheese and sherry vinegar

Pardina lentils, from Castilla y León, are brown lentils that don't lose their skin or their bite. Use Puy lentils as an alternative.

Serves 4

12 oz pardina lentils

6 garlic cloves, 3 finely chopped and 3 left whole

3 fresh bay leaves

6 tablespoons extra-virgin olive oil, plus extra to serve

2 medium red onions, finely chopped

1½ teaspoons superfine sugar

4 oz sun-dried tomatoes in oil, drained and chopped

12 scallions, thinly sliced

3 tablespoons chopped flat-leaf parsley

2 tablespoons sweet Pedro Ximenez, or balsamic sherry vinegar, plus extra to serve

5–7 oz soft rindless goat cheese, sliced

sea salt and freshly ground black pepper

Put the lentils, the 3 whole garlic cloves, and the bay leaves into a pan. and cover with 2 inches cold water. Bring to a boil, and simmer for 20 minutes. Add 1 teaspoon salt, and continue to cook for another 10 minutes, until the lentils are just tender, but still a little *al punto*—with a little bite. Drain, reserving the cooking liquid. Remove and discard the garlic cloves and bay leaves.

Heat half the olive oil in a deep frying pan, add the onions and sugar, and fry gently for 5–6 minutes until soft. Add the chopped garlic, and fry for another 1–2 minutes. Stir in the warm cooked lentils and ⅔ cup of the cooking liquid, the sun-dried tomatoes, scallions, parsley, reserved vinegar, and salt and pepper to taste. Bring back to a gentle simmer.

Spoon the lentils into shallow bowls, and crumble the goat cheese slices on top. Drizzle over a little olive oil and vinegar, and serve.

Garlic shrimp salad with Ibérico ham

Ibérico ham from Extremadura, in my biased opinion, is the best ham in the world. When I have a slice of it, I am transported to a spiritual place!

Serves 4

4 oz prepared chicory

1 tablespoon extra-virgin olive oil

20 large raw peeled shrimp

2 garlic cloves, finely chopped

pinch of crushed dried red pepper flakes

1 red chili pepper, seeded and finely chopped

8 thin slices of Ibérico ham

sea salt and freshly ground black pepper

For the vinaigrette

3 tablespoons extra-virgin olive oil

1 tablespoon Pedro Ximenez sherry vinegar

½ teaspoon superfine sugar

For the vinaigrette, whisk the olive oil with the vinegar, sugar, and some salt and pepper to taste. Put the chicory into a large bowl.

Heat a large frying pan over medium-high heat. Add the olive oil and the shrimp, and season with some salt and pepper. Fry them for 1½ minutes on each side until just cooked through, adding the garlic, red pepper flakes, and fresh chili pepper to the pan as you turn them over.

Pour the vinaigrette over the chicory and toss well together. Adjust the seasoning if necessary, and divide between 4 plates. Arrange the shrimp and ham slices alongside, and serve.

"Poor man's potatoes" with onions, peppers, garlic, and thyme

This is traditionally fried in a large pan, but I find it easier to make in a large roasting pan. It is a great side dish with any roasted or barbecued meat. And, for a quick supper, it is wonderful topped with a couple of fried eggs. When I make this recipe, I always wonder where the name came from—I think it is because the ingredients are so cheap and easily available, and the dish is filling and tasty.

Serves 4

2¼ lb waxy new potatoes
2 large red bell peppers
2 large green bell peppers
3 large red onions, cut into thin wedges
6 fat garlic cloves, thinly sliced
6 fresh bay leaves
leaves from 4 large thyme sprigs
6 tablespoons olive oil
sea salt and freshly ground black pepper

Preheat the oven to 450°F, and bring a large pan of salted water to a boil. Cut the potatoes across into ⅜-inch-thick slices, drop them into the water, bring back to a boil and cook for 1–2 minutes until just tender when pierced with the tip of a knife. Drain well.

Halve the red and green peppers and remove and discard the stalks and seeds. Cut them into ½-inch-wide strips. Put them into a large roasting pan (measuring about 12 x 16 inches) with the potatoes, onions, garlic, bay leaves, and thyme leaves. Season with 2 teaspoons sea salt and plenty of black pepper, pour over 4 tablespoons of the olive oil, and toss well together. Spread everything out in a single even layer, and drizzle over the rest of the olive oil.

Roast on the top shelf of the oven for 20 minutes, then remove the pan, and turn the vegetables over. Return to the oven, and roast for another 20 minutes, until the potatoes are golden, and the other vegetables are tender, and nicely caramelized here and there. Serve immediately.

Seafood, potato, and leek stew with saffron

Potatoes and saffron are a heavenly combination, and this rich, warming stew is a favorite of mine. The best saffron in the world grows in La Mancha and is used in many, many dishes in the center of Spain. They call it "oro rojo" —red gold. It is different from other saffrons because it is toasted on very low heat over a fire. It adds warmth, color and depth to a dish, but be careful not to use too much of it as the subtlety will be lost.

Serves 4

16 large raw unpeeled shrimp

4 tablespoons olive oil

3 fresh bay leaves

6 black peppercorns

14 oz piece of white fish fillet, such as haddock or cod

1 medium onion, chopped

2–3 garlic cloves, finely chopped

1 green bell pepper, seeded and chopped

10 oz leeks, thickly sliced

½ teaspoon saffron strands

1 lb floury potatoes, such as Russet, cut into ¾-inch pieces

2 tablespoons chopped flat-leaf parsley

sea salt

Peel the shrimp, reserving the heads and shells. Heat 2 teaspoons of the oil in a medium pan, add the shrimp heads and shells and sauté them for 2–3 minutes. Add 3½ cups water, the bay leaves, peppercorns, and ½ teaspoon of salt and leave to simmer for 15 minutes. Strain, and return to the pan. Add the fish, cover and simmer for 8 minutes until just cooked through. Lift the fish onto a plate, and strain the stock into a large measuring cup. You should be left with about 2½ cups. Flake the fish, discarding the skin and any bones, and set aside with the stock.

Heat the remaining olive oil in a clean pan, add the onion and garlic, cover, and fry gently until soft, but not browned. Add the green pepper and leeks, cover again, and fry gently for another 3–4 minutes. Stir in the saffron, potatoes, shrimp stock, and another ½ teaspoon salt, bring to a simmer, cover once more, and cook gently for 15 minutes until the potatoes are tender.

Crush some of the potatoes into the stew to thicken it a little, then stir in the shrimp and flaked fish. Simmer for 2 minutes, until the shrimp are cooked through. Adjust the seasoning to taste, stir in the parsley and serve.

Paprika-dusted monkfish on a warm potato, tomato, and basil salad

Sweet paprika (*pimentón dulce*) is not normally used to marinate fish, but I use it for monkfish because of its meaty flavor. *Pimentón de la Vera* is made very close to my home town in Extremadura and is an ingredient I simply couldn't live without. The tomato and basil salad adds a refreshing lightness to the dish.

Serves 4

4 x 6-oz pieces of thick monkfish fillet

½ teaspoon sweet paprika

2 tablespoons olive oil

sea salt and freshly ground black pepper

basil sprigs, to garnish

For the warm potato salad

1¼ lb waxy new potatoes

6 tablespoons extra-virgin olive oil

2 tablespoons red wine vinegar

2 tablespoons wholegrain mustard

7 oz vine-ripened tomatoes, skinned, seeded and diced

6 scallions, thinly sliced

4 green queen olives, pitted and cut lengthwise into thin strips

small handful of basil leaves, finely shredded

Preheat the oven to 400°F. Season the monkfish with salt and set aside for 15 minutes.

Put the potatoes into a pan of cold salted water, bring to a boil and cook for 10–12 minutes or until tender. Meanwhile, pat the monkfish dry on paper towels, then sprinkle each piece generously all over with the paprika. Heat the olive oil in an ovenproof frying pan, add the monkfish pieces and leave them to fry for 1½ minutes. Turn the pieces over, transfer the frying pan to the oven, and roast for 10–12 minutes.

Returning to the potato salad, put the olive oil, vinegar and mustard into a large shallow pan and warm through over low heat. Drain the potatoes, and as soon as you can handle them, quickly cut them into ¾-inch pieces. Add them to the warm dressing with the tomatoes, scallions, and olives, and turn over gently, until everything is coated with the dressing, and heated through.

Remove the monkfish from the oven and carve each piece crosswise into thick slices. Stir the shredded basil into the potato salad with some seasoning to taste, and spoon it onto 4 warmed plates. Place the monkfish alongside, garnish with the basil sprigs, and serve.

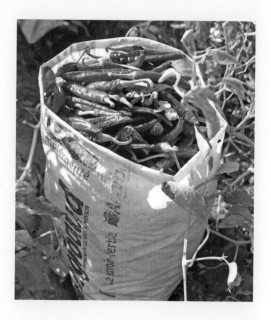

Roasted monkfish with Serrano ham, black olives, and thyme

Monkfish can carry other strong flavors easily, and this combination is stunning. I always use *negra cacereña* olives as they are from my region, and together with the thyme they remind me of my lovely Extremadura. If you can't find *negra cacereña*, use proper, ripe black olives, not the ones that have been oxidized. They should have a lovely oiliness, not a dry, metallic flavor.

Serves 4

6 tablespoons good-quality pitted black olives, finely chopped

1½ teaspoons finely chopped thyme leaves

2 anchovy fillets in olive oil, drained and finely chopped

1 garlic clove, finely chopped

4 x 6-oz pieces of thick monkfish fillet

8 thin slices of Serrano ham

2 tablespoons olive oil, plus extra to serve

sea salt and coarsely ground black pepper

watercress sprigs, to garnish

Preheat the oven to 400°F. Mix together the black olives, thyme, anchovies, and garlic. Cut a pocket lengthwise into each piece of monkfish, taking care not to cut all the way through, and push an equal amount of the black olive mixture into each one. Pat the monkfish dry, season lightly with salt and pepper, then wrap each piece in 2 slices of the ham, securing the parcel at each end with string.

Heat the olive oil in an ovenproof frying pan. Add the ham-wrapped monkfish parcels, and cook for 1½ minutes. Turn the parcels over, transfer the pan to the oven, and roast for 10–12 minutes, until cooked through.

Remove the monkfish from the oven, and lift onto a board. Remove the string. Cut each piece diagonally in half, and arrange on 4 warmed plates. Drizzle a little oil around the outside of each plate, sprinkle with sea salt and some black pepper, and serve garnished with the watercress.

Pan-fried tilapia with caramelized endive, crisp-fried ham, and mint

Where I grew up, we only ever used olive oil for cooking, which is why not many of my recipes are made with butter, but for this dish, using butter with the olive oil to cook the endive takes away its bitterness to achieve a wonderful caramelized flavor.

Serves 4

6 small heads of Belgian endive
2 tablespoons butter
4 tablespoons olive oil
4 teaspoons superfine sugar
1 tablespoon lemon juice
8 thin slices of Serrano ham
4 x 7-oz thick, unskinned tilapia fillets, halved
4 large fresh mint leaves, finely shredded
sea salt and freshly ground black pepper

Remove a layer of outer leaves from each head of endive if they are damaged and trim the base if brown, but take care not to cut off too much, or the leaves will separate. Cut each head in half lengthwise through the base.

Heat the butter and 2 tablespoons of the oil in a large nonstick frying pan, add the endive pieces and fry them for 3 minutes on each side until golden brown. Sprinkle over half the sugar, turn over and cook for another 2 minutes. Sprinkle over the rest of the sugar, turn over once more, and cook for another 2 minutes. Sprinkle over the lemon juice and some seasoning to taste, and fry for a final 2 minutes, until the endive is tender and nicely caramelized.

While the endive is cooking, heat the remaining oil in another frying pan. Add 4 slices of the ham and fry them for 1 minute on each side until nicely golden. Lift onto a tray lined with paper towels, and repeat with the remaining ham.

Season the pieces of tilapia, add them to the frying pan, skin-side down, and fry in the ham-flavored oil for 2½–3 minutes on each side, pressing down on the pieces with a fish spatula as they cook, so that each side browns evenly.

Place 3 pieces of endive into the center of each plate and sprinkle them with the mint. Place the tilapia fillets on top. Tuck 2 slices of crisp ham under each piece of fish, spoon some of the caramelized endive juices around the edge of the plate, and serve.

Pork chops with roasted vinegar onions

The quality of the meat is so important for pork chops, and that you cook them so they are juicy and succulent, not tired and dry. As everyone knows, I think Ibérico pork is the best, but, wherever you are, try to find local, free-range pork to get that superior flavor. Ibérico pork is now found on menus in good restaurants across the world—I even saw it on a menu in Hong Kong earlier this year—and thank you, Peter for taking me there.

Serves 4

4 large pork chops on the bone, ideally
   Ibérico, cut 1-inch thick

2 large garlic cloves

1 teaspoon sweet paprika

3 tablespoons olive oil

2 tablespoons dry white wine

sea salt and freshly ground black pepper

1 quantity Olive Oil Mashed Potatoes (see
   page 33), to serve

For the vinegar onions

2¼ lb red onions

3 tablespoons olive oil

3 tablespoons sherry vinegar

1 tablespoon superfine sugar

1 tablespoon honey

Trim the rind from each pork chop, leaving behind the fatty edge if you wish, then lightly score the meat on both sides into a diamond pattern. Flatten the garlic cloves on a board, sprinkle with ½ teaspoon salt, and crush into a smooth paste with the blade of a large knife. Mix with the paprika, olive oil, white wine, and a little more sea salt and some black pepper. Rub this mixture over both sides of each chop (but try not to get any on the fatty edge) and set aside in the fridge, for at least 1 hour, or overnight.

Preheat the oven to 425°F. Cut the red onions into quarters through the root end, then cut each piece into thin wedges. Put them into a large roasting pan with the olive oil, sherry vinegar, sugar, and some salt and pepper, and toss well together. Roast for 45–50 minutes, removing from the oven and turning them over every 10–15 minutes, until they are soft and nicely caramelized.

About 15 minutes before the onions are ready, heat a large flat griddle or heavy-based frying pan over high heat until smoking hot. Reduce the heat to medium, and, using tongs, hold the chops with their fatty edges on the hot griddle and cook for a couple of minutes until crisp and golden brown. Then lay them flat and sear for 1–2 minutes on each side until nicely browned. Transfer them to a roasting pan in which they will fit side by side, and roast for 8 minutes or until cooked through, but still juicy in the center. Remove from the oven, cover with foil, and leave them to rest for 5 minutes.

Remove the onions from the oven, and stir in the honey and a little more seasoning to taste. Serve with the pork chops and olive oil mashed potatoes.

Fried potatoes, eggs, and ham

My friend Bea Blaquez makes the best *huevos fritos rotos* in the world. Her secret is to use the very best ham, and always the very best olive oil in which to fry the potatoes. This is the ideal dish to have late in the evening with a glass of good red wine.

Serves 2

1 lb Russet potatoes
2½ cups extra-virgin olive oil
4 large free-range eggs
3 oz slice of Ibérico or Serrano ham, cut into small dice
sea salt and freshly ground black pepper

Cut the potatoes lengthwise into ¼-inch-thick slices, then cut the slices lengthwise into thin fries. Pour the oil into a large deep frying pan and heat to 350°F. Add the fries, stir well and leave them to fry for 7–8 minutes, until they are tender and golden brown.

Shortly before the fries are ready, spoon 2 large spoonfuls of the hot oil into another frying pan. Heat the oil until it just starts to smoke, then crack in the eggs, keeping them as far apart as you can, and fry them until the whites are set and the edges nice and crispy.

Lift the fries out of the oil, and drain briefly on plenty of paper towels. Season with salt and pepper and divide between 2 plates. Put the eggs on top, scatter over the ham and eat immediately.

Braised Ibérico pork with tomatoes, chorizo, thyme, and black olives

Pork shoulder is the perfect cut for braising and it's good value for money. This is another recipe that showcases beautiful ingredients from the central area of Spain and how well they combine to create earthy, flavorsome dishes. Serve with *patatas fritas* (fried potatoes) for a wholesome meal.

Serves 4–6

2¼ lb boned shoulder of pork, ideally Ibérico, cut into 1¼-inch chunks

4 tablespoons olive oil

⅔ cup red wine

2 medium onions, chopped

6 garlic cloves, finely chopped

7 oz chorizo sausage, skinned and chopped

2 teaspoons sweet paprika

2 tablespoons tomato paste

14 oz skinned, chopped tomatoes, fresh or canned

1¼ cups chicken stock

leaves from 3 large thyme sprigs

2 tablespoons chopped fresh marjoram or oregano

4 fresh bay leaves

3 tablespoons sherry vinegar

2 teaspoons superfine sugar

3½ oz good-quality pitted black olives

sea salt and freshly ground black pepper

1 quantity *patatas fritas* (see page 117), to serve

Season the pork with salt and pepper. Heat 2 tablespoons of the oil in a large, flameproof casserole, and sear the pork in batches until nicely browned. Set aside in a bowl. Add the wine to the pan, and as the liquid bubbles up, scrape the base of the pan with a wooden spoon to release all the caramelized juices. Pour over the pork.

Add the remaining oil to the pan with the onions, cover and fry gently for 15 minutes, stirring occasionally, until they are very soft and lightly browned. Add the garlic and chorizo, and fry for another 2–3 minutes. Stir in the paprika and cook for 1 minute, then add the tomato paste, tomatoes, chicken stock, thyme leaves, marjoram or oregano, and the bay leaves. Stir in the pork and all the juices, season with salt and pepper, cover, and simmer gently for 1 hour until the pork is almost tender.

Put the sherry vinegar and superfine sugar into a small pan, and boil until reduced to about 1 teaspoon. Stir it into the casserole with the olives and simmer, uncovered, for another 20–30 minutes until the sauce is nicely reduced and the pork is tender. Adjust the seasoning to taste, and serve with the *patatas fritas*.

Clear chicken and vegetable soup with roasted garlic croûtes

The bread is very important for this dish—you need a rustic-style loaf with a crusty exterior and densely textured crumb, and lots of flavor. This is classic comfort food for a cold wintery day. The garlic from La Mancha has a subtle sweet flavor that works well with the soup.

Serves 4

2 heads of garlic
2 tablespoons extra-virgin olive oil, plus extra to serve (optional)
4 chicken thighs
2 large carrots, sliced
2 leeks, thinly sliced
4 celery stalks, sliced
3 fresh bay leaves
8 black peppercorns
5 oz smoked pancetta cubes
1 medium onion, halved and thinly sliced
1½ teaspoons sweet paprika
7 oz vine-ripened tomatoes, skinned, seeded and chopped
4 x ½-inch-thick slices of crusty white bread
sea salt and freshly ground black pepper

Preheat the oven to 400°F. Remove the outer layer of papery skin from each head of garlic and take a thin slice off the top of each one to expose the cloves. Tear off 2 squares of foil, place a head of garlic into the center of each one, drizzle each with 1 teaspoon of the olive oil, and sprinkle with a little salt. Wrap securely in the foil, place in a small roasting pan and roast for 1 hour, until the garlic feels soft when pressed.

Meanwhile, put the chicken thighs into a pan with 1 of the sliced carrots, 1 of the sliced leeks, 1 of the sliced stalks of celery, the bay leaves, peppercorns and 5 cups cold water. Bring to a boil, cover, and leave to simmer gently for 1 hour.

Strain the stock into a bowl, reserving the chicken thighs but discarding the vegetables. Remove the chicken meat from the bones, discarding the skin, and set aside.

Heat the remaining olive oil in a medium pan, add the pancetta, and fry gently until golden. Add the onion, and continue to fry over medium heat until it is soft and lightly golden. Stir in the paprika, and fry for another minute, then stir in the remaining sliced carrot, leek, and celery, Cover, and cook gently for 5–6 minutes. Uncover, add the chicken stock and some seasoning, and simmer for 5 minutes until the vegetables are just tender. Stir in the chicken meat and tomatoes, and adjust the seasoning to taste.

Lightly toast the slices of bread, then singe them over a gas flame, if you can, for a little extra flavor. Spread each one with some of the roasted garlic purée, drizzle with a little olive oil and sprinkle lightly with some sea salt. Place a slice of toast into the bottom of each of 4 warmed soup plates, ladle the soup on top and serve, drizzled with a little extra olive oil if you wish.

Grilled marinated quail with lentil, chorizo, and garlic stew

I have such a vivid memory of seeing quail running through the lentil fields in Extremadura when I was younger. This recipe marries some of the best ingredients of the region—you can tell they have been combined for centuries because they naturally work so well together.

Serves 4

8 quail

For the marinade

4 garlic cloves

2 tablespoons olive oil

3 tablespoons lemon juice

1 teaspoon hot paprika

2 teaspoons cumin seeds, lightly crushed

sea salt and freshly ground black pepper

For the lentil, chorizo, and garlic stew

10 oz pardina or Puy lentils

4 tablespoons olive oil

10 oz cooking chorizo sausage, skinned and chopped

¾ cup shallots, finely chopped

8 garlic cloves, thinly sliced

1 large carrot (7 oz), finely chopped

2 celery stalks, finely chopped

1 tablespoon chopped oregano or marjoram

⅔ cup dry white wine

7 oz skinned, chopped tomatoes, fresh or canned

⅔ cup good-quality chicken stock

Put the quail breast-side down on a board, and cut along either side of the backbone with kitchen scissors and remove. Open up each quail, turn over and press down on the breast bone to make them lie flat.

Use the blade of a large knife to crush the garlic for the marinade to a smooth paste with a little salt. Mix the olive oil, lemon juice, paprika, garlic, and crushed cumin seeds in a large shallow dish. Add the quail, and rub the marinade well into each bird. Set aside to marinate for 1 hour.

Put the lentils into a pan and cover with cold water. Bring to a boil, and simmer for 25–30 minutes, adding 1 teaspoon salt 5 minutes before the end of the cooking time, until just tender but still slightly *al punto*—with a little bite. Drain, reserving the cooking liquid.

For the lentil stew, heat the olive oil in a saucepan over medium heat. Add the chorizo, and fry for 1 minute, stirring. Add the shallots, garlic, carrot, and celery, cover, and fry gently for 15 minutes until soft and lightly browned. Uncover, add the marjoram or oregano, and fry for another minute, then add the wine, and simmer vigorously until it has almost disappeared.

Add the tomatoes and chicken stock, bring to a boil, and simmer for 5 minutes, until the mixture has slightly reduced and thickened. Stir in the cooked lentils and some seasoning to taste, and keep hot.

Heat a ridged cast-iron griddle over high heat until it is smoking hot, then reduce the heat to medium. Season the quail with salt, put them skin-side down onto the griddle, and cook for 5–7 minutes on each side until nicely browned and cooked through. Work in batches if necessary. Stir some of the reserved lentil cooking liquid into the lentil stew if it seems a bit dry, and serve with the griddled quail on top.

Confit of pheasant with sautéed red cabbage, raisins, and pine nuts

Hunting is a much-loved pastime for the locals, and so game in the central regions is abundant. Pheasant shouldn't be too hard to find—ask your local butcher, or visit a farmers' market. The pine nuts from Castille are exceptional, and have a sweetness and aroma that transports you to that area. You can use the breast meat of the pheasants with *planchada* (white kidney) beans for a delicious simple supper.

Serves 4

For the pheasant confit

3½ oz coarse sea salt
½ teaspoon coarsely crushed black pepper
leaves from 3 thyme sprigs
6 juniper berries
8 large, plump pheasant legs
2¼ lb duck or goose fat

For the sautéed red cabbage

¾ cup raisins
4 tablespoons Pedro Ximenez sherry vinegar
3 tablespoons olive oil
1 medium onion, halved and thinly sliced
2 garlic cloves, crushed
1¼ lb red cabbage, quartered, cored and thinly sliced
½ teaspoon ground cumin
½ teaspoon ground coriander
1 tablespoon honey
3 tablespoons pine nuts, toasted
sea salt and freshly ground black pepper

For the pheasant confit, put the salt, pepper, thyme leaves, and juniper berries into a food processor, and grind them together. Place the pheasant legs skin-side down in a shallow china dish, and sprinkle over half of the salt. Turn them over, and sprinkle over the rest of the salt. Cover and refrigerate for 4–5 hours.

Preheat the oven to 275°F. Rub the salt off the pheasant legs, and pat them dry. Melt the duck or goose fat in a flameproof casserole in which the legs will fit quite snugly. Add the pheasant legs, making sure they are completely submerged, bring to a simmer, cover with a lid, and transfer to the oven. Cook for 1½ hours, or until the meat is very tender, but not falling off the bone. Remove from the oven, and if using immediately, shake off the excess fat and place the legs skin-side up in a roasting pan.

If not using immediately, refrigerate until the fat is hard, then carefully lift out the legs encased in fat, and scrape away and discard (or save for stock) the jelly-like pheasant juices from the base of the pan. Return the legs encased in fat to the pan, place it on the heat, and leave until the fat has melted again. Push the pheasant legs under the surface, turn off the heat, leave to cool and refrigerate until needed. Then ease the legs out of the fat, scrape away the excess, and put them skin-side up into a roasting pan.

Preheat the oven to 400°F. Roast the pheasant legs for 15–20 minutes until heated through, and the skin is golden brown.

Meanwhile, make the red cabbage. Put the raisins and 3 tablespoons of the sherry vinegar into a small pan, and warm gently over low heat. Remove and set aside. Heat the oil in a medium pan. Add the onion, and fry for 5 minutes until soft and lightly browned. Add the garlic and fry for 2 minutes, then add the cabbage and stir-fry for 5 minutes. Add the cumin, coriander, and some seasoning, reduce the heat, cover, and leave to cook for 8–10 minutes, giving it a stir every now and then, until tender.

Stir the vinegar-soaked raisins and the honey into the cabbage, and cook for another 2 minutes. Stir in the remaining vinegar, and some salt and pepper to taste, then stir in the pine nuts. Serve with the pheasant.

Venison, red wine, and chestnut stew

When we were filming with Rick Stein in Extremadura, we went to Marques de Valduza to hunt deer, but we didn't end up shooting any, and so settled for a delicious *ajo blanco* (white garlic) soup instead. Extremadura is abundant with chestnut trees, and they are used in many different recipes. The nuttiness goes well with the gamey flavor of the venison. A *tempranillo* from the area would be perfect to use as your red wine in the recipe and to drink with it.

Serves 4–6

2¼ lb stewing venison, preferably from the leg or haunch

3 tablespoons flour

5 tablespoons olive oil

4 tablespoons sherry vinegar

5 oz pancetta or dry-cured bacon, cut into short fat strips

1 medium onion, halved and thinly sliced

4 garlic cloves, crushed

1¼ cups game or beef stock

7 fl oz robust red wine, such as *tempranillo*

1 teaspoon tomato paste

3½ fl oz sweet sherry, such as Oloroso

leaves from 3 large thyme sprigs

1 teaspoon juniper berries, lightly crushed

2 tablespoons clear honey

7 oz baby onions, peeled

7 oz cooked, peeled chestnuts

sea salt and freshly ground black pepper

1 quantity *patatas fritas* (see page 117) or Olive Oil Mashed Potatoes (see page 33), to serve

Cut the venison into 1½-inch pieces. Coat them lightly in the flour, reserving the excess. Heat 2 tablespoons of the oil in a large, flameproof casserole over medium-high heat. Brown the venison in batches, spooning it into a bowl as each batch is done.

Pour away the excess oil from the casserole, add the vinegar to the pan and scrape the base with a wooden spoon as the liquid bubbles, to release all the caramelized juices. Pour over the venison in the bowl.

Add another tablespoon of the oil and the pancetta to the casserole and fry for 2 minutes until lightly golden. Remove with a slotted spoon and add to the venison. Add another tablespoon of the oil and the onion, and fry for 7–8 minutes, stirring frequently, until soft and richly golden. Add the garlic, and cook for 2 minutes. Stir in any remaining flour, followed by the game or beef stock, red wine, tomato paste, sherry, thyme leaves, juniper berries, and honey. Bring to a boil, stirring. Return the venison, pancetta, and all the juices to the casserole, season with salt and pepper, and stir well. Cover and leave to simmer gently for 1 hour.

Meanwhile, heat the remaining oil in a small pan, add the baby onions and fry, shaking the pan occasionally, until they are nicely browned all over. Uncover the casserole, and stir in the baby onions and the chestnuts. Simmer for another 25 minutes until the meat is tender. Leave the casserole uncovered if the liquid needs to reduce and thicken a little more. Serve with *patatas fritas* or olive oil mashed potatoes.

Hunter's rice with rabbit and wild herbs

It is best to prepare the rabbit in advance so that you can make a stock from the bones. In my area, there used to be many more hares than rabbits (although it's the opposite these days), so this dish was made with hare and ingredients that the hunter would have readily. Here we use farmed rabbit, but if you're lucky enough to get a wild rabbit the cooking time will be about 20 minutes longer. If neither is available, you can substitute chicken.

Serves 4–6

pinch of saffron strands

1 quart rabbit or chicken stock

6 oz green beans, trimmed

1 farmed rabbit (or 1½ lb chicken), cut into small pieces through the bone

3 tablespoons olive oil

1 medium onion, finely chopped

4 garlic cloves, finely chopped

½ teaspoon sweet paprika (optional)

¼ teaspoon crushed dried red pepper flakes

10 oz vine-ripened tomatoes, skinned and chopped

leaves from 2 large fresh thyme sprigs

leaves from a 4-inch rosemary sprig, chopped

leaves from 2 large wild oregano sprigs, chopped

6 small fresh bay leaves

14 oz paella rice (preferably Calasparra)

10-oz jar artichoke hearts in olive oil, drained and cut into quarters

sea salt and freshly ground black pepper

Bring a pan of salted water to a boil. Shake the saffron around in a hot, dry frying pan for a few seconds, then pour into a mortar, and grind to a fine powder. Transfer the saffron powder to a pan, add the stock, and bring to a boil, then remove from the heat and set aside. Drop the green beans into the boiling water, and cook for 3 minutes. Drain, refresh under cold water, and set aside.

Season the rabbit (or chicken) pieces with salt and pepper. Heat the olive oil in a 15-inch paella pan, or large, deep frying pan over medium heat, add the meat, and fry until golden brown all over. Lift onto a plate and set aside.

Add the onion to the pan, and fry for 6–7 minutes until soft and lightly golden. Add the garlic, paprika (if using), and the red pepper flakes, and fry for 1 minute. Add the tomatoes, and cook for 2 minutes. Stir in the herbs, and cook for another 2 minutes. Add the stock, and bring to a boil. Taste the stock, and season with salt and plenty of pepper.

Pour in the rice, and stir so that it is evenly distributed in the pan. Place the rabbit (or chicken) pieces around the pan with the artichokes, and shake the pan gently so the pieces bed down into the rice. Scatter over the green beans, and leave to simmer vigorously for 6 minutes. Then reduce the heat and leave to cook undisturbed for 14–15 minutes, until all the liquid has been absorbed, and the rice is *al punto*—still with a little bite. Turn off the heat, cover the pan with a clean cloth, and leave it to rest for 5 minutes before serving.

Slow-cooked beans with partridge, bacon, and garlic

This recipe originated in Castile, but the combination of beans and partridge is used all over Spain. The beans and the partridge have different cooking times, so for this dish, it is better to cook them separately. My mother used to prepare a recipe like this after my brother and I had been shooting the first partridge in the autumn, but I have added some pancetta to bring a bit of fattiness and therefore extra flavor. This is a great dinner-party dish for the autumn months.

Serves 4

7 tablespoons olive oil
2 medium onions, chopped
1 small head of garlic, separated into cloves, and finely chopped
¼ teaspoon crushed dried red pepper flakes
14 dried white beans, such as *alubia planchada (white kidney beans)*, soaked in water overnight
1 fresh bay leaf
4 oven-ready partridges (or 6 quail)
7 oz bacon or pancetta, diced
2 green bell peppers, seeded and thinly sliced
1 teaspoon sweet paprika
⅔ cup dry white wine
3 cups good-quality chicken stock
sea salt and freshly ground black pepper
1 tablespoon chopped flat-leaf parsley, to serve

For the slow-cooked beans, heat 3 tablespoons of the oil in a large saucepan, add 1 of the chopped onions, half the chopped garlic and the red pepper flakes, cover, and fry gently for 10 minutes until soft and lightly golden. Drain and rinse the beans, add them to the pan with the bay leaf, and cover with 1 quart cold water. Bring to a gentle simmer, reduce the heat to low, partially cover, and leave to cook for 2 hours until the liquid has reduced and almost disappeared, and the beans are very tender.

Meanwhile, cut the partridges in half lengthwise, through the backbone and breastbone, using kitchen scissors, and clean them well of any stray feathers or bits of gut. Season all over with salt and pepper.

Heat the remaining oil in a flameproof casserole over medium heat. Add the partridge halves and fry them until golden brown all over. Lift them onto a plate and set aside.

Add the bacon or pancetta to the pan, and fry for 2 minutes until lightly golden. Add the remaining chopped onion and garlic, and the green peppers, and cook for 5 minutes until soft. Stir in the paprika, followed by the wine, and leave it to bubble away until reduced by half. Return the partridges to the pan with the stock, bring back to a simmer, partially cover, and cook over low heat for 40–50 minutes, depending on the size of the birds, until they are quite tender, and the liquid has reduced by about half.

Strip the meat off the bones if you wish (simply to make this dish slightly easier to eat). Stir the beans into the partridge stew, adjust the seasoning to taste and bring back to a simmer. Ladle into 4 warmed shallow bowls, and serve sprinkled with the chopped parsley.

Barbecued lamb with honey, mustard, garlic, and rosemary

The honey in the marinade makes the surface of the lamb caramelize to give a fantastic flavor, which contrasts so well with the beautifully tender pink meat inside. We couldn't find neck fillets in La Boqueria, the famous food market in Barcelona, as they don't butcher there in the same way, so we used a seam-boned leg of lamb instead. This is wonderful served with the lentil salad on page 132 or the "poor man's potatoes" on page 109.

Serves 4

4 x 8-oz lamb neck fillets or 1 small leg
  of lamb, seam-boned

For the marinade

3 fat garlic cloves

4 tablespoons honey

1 tablespoon wholegrain mustard

leaves from 2 x 4-inch rosemary sprigs,
  finely chopped

2 tablespoons olive oil

1½ tablespoons lemon juice

sea salt and freshly ground black pepper

For the marinade, use the blade of a large knife to crush the garlic to a smooth paste with a little salt. Mix together the honey, mustard, garlic, rosemary, olive oil, lemon juice, and some pepper in a shallow dish. Add the lamb neck fillets or boned lamb leg, cut into 4 pieces, turn them over in the mixture to coat well and leave to marinate for at least 1 hour.

Preheat your barbecue to medium-high. Lift the lamb fillets out of the marinade and shake off the excess. Season with salt and a little more pepper. Barbecue the lamb fillets for 5 minutes on each side, basting once or twice with the leftover marinade, until nicely browned on the outside and slightly pink in the center. Some pieces of the boned lamb will take a little longer, so barbecue until the center of the meat registers 140°F on a meat thermometer. Lift the fillets onto a board, wrap tightly in foil and leave them to rest for 4–5 minutes. Then slice thickly and serve immediately.

Chargrilled leg of lamb with a fennel and lentil salad

This is a wonderful recipe to barbecue, but you can get the same effect by starting it off on a large ridged grill pan to give it a good color and smoky flavor, then transfering to the oven in a roasting dish to finish it off. A winter alternative to fennel is radicchio, giving an extra bitterness to the dish.

Serves 6

1 x 5½ lb leg of lamb, butterflied

sea salt

For the marinade

6 tablespoons olive oil

leaves from 1 large rosemary sprig, finely
    chopped

2 large garlic cloves, crushed

finely grated zest and juice of 1 small lemon

½ teaspoon coarsely crushed black
    peppercorns

For the fennel and lentil salad

1 large fennel bulb

10½ oz green lentils, such as pardina

6 tablespoons extra-virgin olive oil

finely grated zest of ½ lemon and
    2 tablespoons lemon juice

1¼ cups good-quality black olives, pitted

2 tablespoons chopped fennel herb or fronds

For the marinade, mix the oil, rosemary, garlic, lemon zest and juice, pepper, and some of the salt together in a large shallow dish. Add the lamb, turn it over a few times to coat well, then cover and leave to marinate at room temperature for at least 1 hour or in the fridge overnight.

The next day, if you are barbecuing your lamb, preheat the barbecue to high. Alternatively, preheat the oven to 400°F. Meanwhile, make the salad. Thinly slice the fennel bulb on a mandoline, drop the slices into a large bowl of ice water, and leave in the fridge to crisp up. Put the lentils into a pan, cover by 2 inches with cold water, bring to a boil, and simmer for about 25–30 minutes, or until just cooked but still a little *al punto*—with a little bite, adding 1 teaspoon salt 5 minutes before the end of cooking. Meanwhile, whisk together the olive oil, lemon juice, lemon zest, and some salt and pepper to taste. Drain the lentils well, pour into a bowl, and stir in the lemon dressing. Leave to cool.

Season the lamb with salt, place, skin-side down, on the barbecue and cook for 12–15 minutes on each side, moving it around occasionally to avoid any flare-ups. Alternatively, preheat a large ridged grill pan over high heat, reduce the heat slightly, and grill the lamb for 5–7 minutes on each side. Then transfer to a roasting pan, and roast in the oven for 20–25 minutes. The meat is cooked to medium when it registers 140°F at its thickest part. Lift it onto a board, wrap loosely in foil and leave to rest for 5–10 minutes.

To finish the salad, drain the sliced fennel and dry it well in a salad spinner or on a clean kitchen towel. Stir the fennel into the lentils with the black olives, fennel herb, and a little more seasoning to taste. Carve the lamb crosswise into slices, and serve with the salad.

Spiced beef and potato fritters

When I started researching this book, I asked my lovely sister Isabel to find me Spanish cookbooks that had a Jewish influence, and I found this recipe, created by the Jews from north Extremadura. It looks rather elaborate, but it is worth the effort because the fritters taste amazing.

Makes 14 fritters

2¼ lb floury potatoes, such as Russet

1 egg, beaten

olive oil, for shallow-frying

1 cup fresh white breadcrumbs

sea salt and freshly ground black pepper

green salad, to serve

For the filling

1 medium onion, finely chopped

3 tablespoons olive oil

12 oz lean ground beef (or lamb)

seeds from 4 green cardamom pods

1 teaspoon cumin seeds

2 teaspoons coriander seeds

1 teaspoon ground cinnamon

½ teaspoon ground allspice

½ teaspoon sweet paprika

freshly grated nutmeg

3 tablespoons chopped flat-leaf parsley

For the filling, fry the onion in the olive oil for 10 minutes until soft and lightly golden. Add the ground beef and fry for 2–3 minutes, breaking up any lumps with a spoon as it browns. Put the cardamom, cumin, and coriander seeds into a spice grinder and grind to a fine powder. Add to the ground beef mixture with the cinnamon, allspice, paprika, salt, pepper, and 7 fl oz water. Simmer gently, stirring occasionally, until all the liquid has evaporated. Pour into a sieve set over a bowl, and drain away the excess oil. Return to the pan, stir in the nutmeg and parsley, and adjust the seasoning if necessary. Allow to cool.

Meanwhile, cut the potatoes into large chunks, put into a pan of salted water, bring to a boil, and cook for 20 minutes, or until tender. Drain well, leave until the steam dies down, then return to the pan and mash until smooth. Stir in the beaten egg and some salt and pepper to taste. Leave until cool enough to handle.

Lightly oil your hands and shape a tangerine-sized piece (2½ oz) of mashed potato into a flat 4-inch disk. Put a tablespoon of the meat mixture into the center, and wrap the potato around it to form a ball. Seal any gaps, then flatten gently into a 2¾-inch patty. Repeat with the remaining filling and mashed potato. The patties can be prepared up to this point in advance.

Heat ½ inch of olive oil in a large frying pan over medium heat to 325°F. Coat half of the fritters in the breadcrumbs, add them to the pan, and fry for 5 minutes on each side until crisp and golden. Lift onto a tray lined with paper towels, and keep warm while you coat and cook the remainder. Serve with a lightly dressed green leaf salad.

Pan-fried lamb's brains on toast with leaves and walnut oil dressing

My mother used to cook me lamb's brains, just blanched and deep-fried in a simple batter, served with toasted bread. Sometimes we would have them in scrambled eggs—they were delicious. You can find lamb's brains in specialty butchers.

Serves 4

2 lamb's brains
4 tablespoons olive oil
1 tablespoon cold-pressed walnut oil
2½ teaspoons good-quality white wine vinegar
4 large or 8 small slices of brown walnut bread, ½ inch thick
2 tablespoons butter
½ oak leaf lettuce, broken into leaves
¼ cup walnut pieces, lightly toasted
sea salt and freshly ground black pepper

Soak the lamb's brains in cold water for 24 hours, changing the water occasionally. Bring 2½ quarts of water to a boil with 1 tablespoon salt. Split each brain into 2 lobes, add them to the boiling water, bring back to a boil, then remove from the heat and leave them to cool in the liquid. This can be done in advance. Remove the membrane, and any veins from the brains. Slice each lobe lengthwise into 3 slices.

Whisk 2 tablespoons of the olive oil, the walnut oil and vinegar together in a small bowl, and season to taste with salt and pepper.

Toast the slices of walnut bread and put onto each plate. Put half the butter and 1 tablespoon of the remaining oil into a large frying pan over high heat, and when the butter foams, add half of the lamb's brain slices, season lightly, and fry for 1 minute on each side. Divide between 2 of the slices of toast. Repeat with the remaining butter, oil, and brains. Toss 1 tablespoon of the salad dressing through the lettuce leaves and scatter them around the plates. Sprinkle with the toasted walnuts, drizzle the remaining dressing over the plates, and serve.

Liver with sweet caramelized onions and slow-cooked grapes

Offal has been popular in the central regions of Spain since the time of Don Quixote and before. It was used because of poverty and necessity. The combination of the earthy flavor of the liver and the sweetness of the onions and grapes is delicious. Muscatel grapes would be really lovely in this recipe.

Serves 4

1 lb small, seedless red grapes
5 tablespoons olive oil
4 medium onions, halved and thinly sliced
14 oz lamb's liver, cut into 8 slices, ½-inch thick
3 tablespoons sweet sherry, such as Pedro Ximenez
2 teaspoons Pedro Ximenez sherry vinegar
sea salt and freshly ground black pepper

Preheat the oven to 400°F. Spread the grapes out on a nonstick baking sheet. Roast for 25–30 minutes, shaking the tray occasionally to prevent them from sticking. Reduce the oven temperature to 275°F and roast for another 40–45 minutes until shriveled, sticky, and sweet. Remove and set aside.

Heat 2 tablespoons of the oil in a large frying pan, add the sliced onions, cover, and cook over medium heat, stirring occasionally, for about 15–20 minutes, until soft and nicely caramelized. Season and set aside.

Season the lamb's liver on both sides. Heat the remaining oil in a large frying pan over medium heat. Add the liver slices and cook for about 20–30 seconds on each side. Lift the lamb's liver onto a warmed plate. Pour away the excess oil from the pan, add the sherry and sherry vinegar, and scrape the base of the pan with a wooden spoon as the liquid bubbles to release all the caramelized juices. Season to taste. Stir in the slow-cooked grapes, and warm through quickly.

To serve, spoon the caramelized onions onto warmed plates, and put the liver on top. Spoon over the sauce and grapes, and serve.

Orange, almond, and pine nut tartlets

These little tarts are so addictive. The flavors combine to create a not-too-sweet pastry that can be savored any time of the day. They are perfect for a dinner party dessert, or warm from the oven for a teatime treat.

Makes 8 individual tartlets or 1 x 9-inch tart

For the pastry

1¾ cups all-purpose flour, plus extra
   for dusting

pinch of salt

½ cup confectioners' sugar

1 stick chilled butter, cut into small pieces

finely grated zest of ½ large orange

1 large egg yolk

4 teaspoons orange juice

For the filling

1½ sticks butter, softened

heaping ¾ cup superfine sugar

finely grated zest of 2 small oranges

2 extra large free-range (cage-free) eggs

heaping ¼ cup self-rising flour

1¾ cups ground almonds

⅔ cup pine nuts, toasted

heaping ¼ cup chopped candied peel, plus
   extra to decorate

4 tablespoons shredless marmalade, to glaze

For the pastry, sift the flour, salt, and confectioners' sugar into a food processor. Add the butter and orange zest, and process briefly until the mixture resembles fine bread crumbs. Beat the egg yolk briefly with the orange juice. Pour the crumbed mixture into a bowl, stir in the egg yolk and orange mixture, and bring the dough together into a ball. Turn out onto a lightly floured surface, and knead briefly until smooth. Chill for 15 minutes, then remove from the fridge and, if making individual tartlets, cut into 8 even-sized pieces. Thinly roll out the pastry, and use to line either 8 lightly buttered 4-inch x 1½-inch deep tartlet cases, or a loose-based 9-inch x 1½-inch deep tart pan. Refrigerate for 20 minutes.

Put a baking sheet on the middle shelf of the oven and preheat it to 400°F. Line the pastry case(s) with foil and a thin layer of baking beans and bake for 15 minutes. Remove the foil and beans and bake for another 3 minutes or until the pastry is crisp and golden brown. Remove from the oven and set aside. Reduce the oven temperature to 325°F.

For the filling, beat the butter, sugar, and orange zest together in a bowl until light and fluffy. Gradually beat in the eggs, adding the flour with the final addition. Fold in the ground almonds, pine nuts, and chopped candied peel. Spoon the mixture into the pastry case(s) and smooth over the tops. Bake in the center of the oven for 25–30 minutes for the individual tarts, or 35–40 minutes for the large tart, until puffed up and golden, and a toothpick, inserted into the center, comes away clean. Remove the tart(s) from the oven and allow to cool for 10 minutes.

Meanwhile, warm the marmalade with 2 teaspoons water in a small pan. Brush the tart(s) generously with the marmalade, scatter with a little extra chopped candied peel, and serve warm or cold.

Broiled figs with goat cheese, honey, and walnuts

This recipe reminds me of my father, because he has figs and walnuts in his garden and makes honey. We used to get goat curd from the local farmer, which was so delicious. Now it is harder to get, so I have used a soft goat cheese instead.

Serves 4

heaping ⅓ cup walnut pieces

8 large fresh figs

3½ oz rindless goat cheese, thinly sliced

3 tablespoons honey

4 large mint leaves, finely shredded

Preheat the broiler to medium-high. Spread the walnuts on a baking sheet and carefully toast them for a minute or two until lightly golden. Remove, and leave to go cold.

Cut a deep cross into the top of each fig, about two-thirds of the way down to the base, and then give them a gentle squeeze, to open them up slightly like a flower. Divide the goat cheese evenly between each fig, and place them on a baking sheet. Broil for 3–4 minutes until the figs are soft, and the cheese is bubbling and lightly golden.

Lift the figs onto plates and drizzle a little honey over each one. Sprinkle with the walnuts and mint before serving.

Velvety chocolate pots with marrons glacés

The most popular way of eating chocolate in Spain is in *churros con chocolate*, **deep-fried lengths of flour and water paste (they are like doughnuts), sometimes dusted in sugar, dipped into small cups of very thick hot chocolate. But I love chocolate any way, and these little pots are my idea of heaven after a good meal. Chestnuts are very popular in Extremadura and so I make this dessert for my sister when I go and visit.**

Makes 6

6 marrons glacés (candied chestnuts)

scant ½ cup whole milk

1¼ cups heavy cream

2½ tablespoons superfine sugar

6 oz good-quality dark chocolate
  (at least 70% cocoa solids)

1½ teaspoons vanilla extract

1 extra large free-range (cage-free) egg,
  beaten

Preheat the oven to 275°F, and put a kettleful of water on to boil. Cut 6 of the marrons glacés into small thin pieces. Divide evenly between 6 x 4-oz heatproof pots or ramekins and put them into a small roasting pan. Slice the remaining marrons glacés and set aside.

Put the milk, cream, and sugar into a small pan, and bring slowly to a boil, stirring once or twice to dissolve the sugar. Meanwhile, break the chocolate into a small mixing bowl. As soon as the milk mixture starts to bubble around the edge of the pan, remove from the heat, leave for 1 minute to cool slightly, then pour onto the chocolate and stir until smooth. Stir in the vanilla extract and beaten egg. Strain the mixture into a pitcher and pour equally into the pots.

Pour hot (but not boiling) water from the kettle into the roasting pan to come halfway up the sides of the pots. Carefully slide the pan into the oven, and cook for 15 minutes, until the pots are almost set, but still have a slight wobble in the center. Remove the pan from the oven, take the pots out of the water, and leave them to cool and set at room temperature, then serve.

Walnut and orange blossom honey tart

This is a perfect tart to make in advance as it lasts for 2 or 3 days easily. I always use orange blossom honey to give a fruity, floral flavor to the tart. You could serve it with ice cream as dessert or on its own for tea.

Serves 8–10 (makes 1 x 9-inch tart)

For the pastry

1¹/₃ cups all-purpose flour

pinch of salt

heaping ¹/₃ cup confectioners' sugar

¾ stick chilled butter, cut into small pieces

finely grated zest of ½ lemon

1 large egg yolk

1 tablespoon cold water

For the filling

5 tablespoons unsalted butter

scant ½ cup light brown sugar

½ cup orange blossom honey

²/₃ cup heavy cream

1½ tablespoons lemon juice

1 extra large egg, beaten

1½ cups walnut halves

For the pastry, sift the flour, salt, and confectioners' sugar into a food processor. Add the butter and lemon zest, and process briefly until the mixture resembles fine bread crumbs. Beat the egg yolk briefly with the water. Pour the crumbed mixture into a bowl, stir in the egg yolk mixture, and bring the dough together into a ball. Turn out onto a lightly floured surface, and knead briefly until smooth. Chill for 15 minutes, then remove from the fridge, thinly roll out into a disk and use to line a 9 x 1½-inch deep, loose-based tart pan. Refrigerate for 20 minutes.

Put a baking sheet on the middle shelf of the oven and preheat it to 400°F. Line the pastry case with foil and a thin layer of baking beans, and bake for 15–20 minutes, until the edges are lightly golden. Remove the foil and beans and bake for another 5–7 minutes, or until the base of the case is crisp and golden brown. Remove and set aside. Reduce the oven temperature to 350°F.

For the filling, melt the butter in a medium pan over low heat. Add the sugar and honey, and stir gently until the sugar has dissolved. Then increase the heat, and simmer vigorously for 4 minutes. Add the cream (be careful as it will splutter a little), and boil for another 3 minutes. Stir in the lemon juice. Remove from the heat, and leave the mixture to cool until just warm, then stir in the beaten egg.

Arrange the walnut halves over the base of the pastry case in an even layer, and pour over the honey and cream mixture. Bake for 30–35 minutes until the filling is set and golden brown. Serve warm, cut into wedges.

THE SOUTH

THE SOUTH: INTRODUCTION

El Andalus was the name the Muslims gave to the southern part of Spain that they conquered and governed for over 700 years, and Andalusia is derived from the Arabic name for their mighty kingdom. It is now the largest of the country's 17 autonomous regions and world-famous for its flamenco, fiestas, and bullfights. The legacy of the Moorish occupation is very much apparent in Andalusia's architecture and culinary traditions, including many exotic ingredients—among them mint, coriander, cinnamon, olives, citrus fruits, including the bitter Seville oranges, figs, dates, eggplant, sugar cane, rice and vines—and Arabic cooking styles, such as the use of dried fruits and honey in savory as well as sweet recipes.

Andalusia is associated in my mind with family holidays, particularly the area around Siempre I can still recall the long trips from Talaván in Extremadura to Cadiz, which took 6 overpoweringly hot hours traveling in the back of a Citroen 2CV. Now, thankfully, the journey is a lot quicker, only 3 hours.

I visit Andalusia, not only for my vacations in Puerto de Santa María, but for my work. The heat and long hours of sunshine make this blessed region the source of great ingredients—seemingly exotic fruit, including pomegranates, persimmons, passion fruit, and a vast array of olives and oils—that I use in my kitchen, and they feature in many of the traditional recipes that I have on the menu in my restaurants, and certainly in my books. Being a chef offers me the perfect excuse to visit the south whenever I can, and stroll through Seville when the orange trees are in bloom, to visit the Alhambra of Granada, or the mosque at Córdoba, witness the horse races along the beach at Sanlúcar de Barrameda, or spend summer nights eating freshly fried fish on a terrace, or enjoy a lazy afternoon with friends moving from one tapas bar to another.

Another of my passions is sherry, the wines of Jerez. There is always a bottle in my kitchen—for drinking and cooking. Many people ask me which sherry wines I use for cooking, and my response is very simple: Manzanilla and Fino, the lightest and driest of the sherry styles, are used in the same way as white wine, while the darker, richer styles such as Palo Cortado and Oloroso can be used in the same way as red wine. Adding sherry to a dish imparts a certain flavor and a very different aroma, which derive from the yeast in the wine. The darkest and sweetest of all sherries, which has been described as "Christmas pudding in a glass," is Pedro Ximenez, an irresistible accompaniment to a dessert but not only to drink with it—try adding a generous spoonful to good vanilla ice cream: simple but amazing.

Crisp, deep-fried eggplant fritters with honey

This is another really good, easy tapas dish that sells very quickly in José. The delicious, subtle flavor of the soft eggplant comes through when it is cooked in this way, and the crispy coating and sticky honey make this a heavenly dish.

Serves 4–6

1 medium eggplant, cut into ¼-inch-thick slices

heaping ¾ cup all-purpose flour

5 tablespoons olive oil, plus extra for deep-frying

⅔ cup cold water

2 free-range (cage-free) egg whites

honey, for drizzling

fine sea salt

Sprinkle the eggplant slices lightly on both sides with salt, and set aside for 30 minutes. Sift the flour into a bowl, make a well in the center, and add the oil and the water. Gradually beat together to make a smooth batter. Set aside to rest, along with the eggplant.

Pat the eggplant slices dry with paper towels. Pour ½ inch of olive oil into a large deep frying pan and heat it to 350°F.

Whisk the egg whites into soft peaks, and fold them into the batter. Dip the eggplant slices, a few at a time, into the batter, add them to the hot oil and deep-fry for 1 minute on each side until crisp and golden. Leave to drain briefly on paper towels, and serve immediately while they are still hot and crisp, drizzled generously with the honey.

Sweet-and-sour Moorish eggplants with chili, garlic, and mint

I always get a call from my friend Tony in Maltby Street market, when the first eggplants have come in. I love to cook this recipe with those first small eggplants, mixing the Moorish herbs and spices with the smoky-tasting vegetables. This recipe is great for lunch or as an appetizer.

Serves 4

18 oz small, thin eggplants

sea salt and freshly ground black pepper

1 scant cup red wine vinegar

3¼ tablespoons superfine sugar

6 tablespoons extra-virgin olive oil

4 garlic cloves, finely chopped

1 medium-hot red chili pepper, seeded and finely chopped

2 tablespoons chopped fresh mint, plus a few small whole leaves to garnish

Halve the eggplants lengthwise (or cut into ½-inch-thick slices if you can find only large ones). Sprinkle lightly on both sides with salt and set aside for 30 minutes.

Put the red wine vinegar and sugar into a small pan, and boil until reduced to ¼ cup. Remove from the heat, and set aside. Put 2 tablespoons of the olive oil and the garlic into a small pan and place it over medium-low heat. As soon as the garlic begins to sizzle, add the red chili pepper, and cook until the garlic is very lightly golden. Stir into the vinegar mixture, and season to taste with salt and pepper.

Heat a ridged cast-iron grill pan over high heat until smoking hot, then reduce the heat to medium. Pat the eggplants dry with paper towels. Brush a few slices at a time with the remaining oil, place on the grill pan and cook for 3 minutes on each side, until browned and tender. Transfer each batch to a shallow serving dish as they are ready.

Stir the chopped mint into the dressing and spoon it over the eggplants. Scatter over a few baby mint leaves and serve warm.

Warm potato soup with shrimp, eggs, and bacalao

This is an unusual but very delicious soup, also known as *sopa de huevos* (egg soup) because it is made from mayonnaise. It is thinned down with the potato cooking water or stock, flavored with vinegar, and traditionally garnished with diced cooked egg white and potatoes, small shrimp, and some flaked white fish or *bacalao*. It's also good served with clams. The flavor will entirely depend on the olive oil that you use for the mayonnaise, so use the very best that you can find. This soup is quite rich, and is therefore usually served only in small portions.

Serves 4

5 oz piece *bacalao* (salt cod), soaked in water for at least 24 hours (see page 44)
2 extra large eggs
9 oz waxy new potatoes
6 oz cooked peeled small shrimp
salt
chopped flat-leaf parsley, to garnish

For the mayonnaise

2 extra large egg yolks
1 tablespoon sherry vinegar
1 cup really good-quality olive oil

First make the mayonnaise. Put the egg yolks into a large mixing bowl, add 2 teaspoons of the vinegar and a good pinch of salt, and very gradually whisk in the olive oil, until you have a smooth, thick mayonnaise. Cover, and set aside.

Put the soaked *bacalao* into a pan, cover with cold water, and bring to a boil over medium heat. Turn off the heat, cover, and leave for 10 minutes. Then lift the fish onto a plate and, when it is cool enough to handle, flake the fish, discarding the skin and any bones. Cover, and set aside.

Hard-boil the eggs for 9 minutes. Meanwhile, cut the potatoes into ¾-inch dice. Put them into a pan with 2½ cups cold water and 1 teaspoon salt. Bring to a boil, cover, and simmer for 3–4 minutes until they are just tender. Drain the potatoes, reserving the cooking water. Leave to cool slightly. Drain the hard-boiled eggs, cover with cold water, and leave to cool. Then peel and cut into small dice.

Whisk 14 fl oz of the potato cooking water into the mayonnaise, pour the mixture into a large pan, and stir over low heat, as you would for a custard, until the mixture thickens, and lightly coats the back of the spoon. Take care not to let it boil. Stir in the remaining sherry vinegar, and season to taste with salt. Stir in the potatoes, flaked *bacalao* and shrimp, and continue to heat gently for another 3–4 minutes, again taking care not to let it boil, until everything has heated through.

Ladle the soup into 4 small warmed bowls, and sprinkle with chopped parsley. Serve immediately.

Spicy vegetable and chorizo pisto with eggs

This is a late summer vegetable stew that you could make to use up a glut of zucchini and tomatoes. I've added chorizo to the classic *pisto* to make it more robust, but you could always leave it out and enjoy this it as a great vegetarian dish—just use a little more paprika for flavor. I've included cumin to give a Moorish influence to the dish.

Serves 2

4 tablespoons olive oil

1 large onion, halved and chopped

1 red bell pepper, seeded and diced

2 garlic cloves, finely chopped

1 teaspoon ground cumin

½ teaspoon crushed dried red pepper flakes

1 medium eggplant, cut into ¾-inch pieces

7 oz zucchini, cut into ½-inch pieces

14 oz skinned, chopped tomatoes, fresh
  or canned

4 large free-range eggs

pinch of hot paprika

sea salt and freshly ground black pepper

Heat the oil in a large frying pan over medium heat. Add the onion and red pepper, cover, and cook gently for 7–8 minutes, until soft and lightly golden. Uncover, stir in the garlic, cumin, and red pepper flakes, and cook for 1 minute. Stir in the eggplant, re-cover, and cook for 4 minutes until beginning to soften, then stir in the zucchini, season with salt, and cook for another 4 minutes. Stir in the tomatoes, ⅔ cup water, and some salt and pepper and simmer for 7–8 minutes, until all the vegetables are tender, and the sauce has reduced and thickened slightly.

Break the eggs on top of the mixture and sprinkle them with some paprika and a little salt. Cover the pan with a tight-fitting lid, and simmer gently for 5 minutes, or until the eggs are set to your liking. Serve with fresh crusty bread.

Salmorejo-style tomato soup with hard-boiled eggs, olives, and crisp-fried ham

This is a rich, thick, and creamy chilled bread soup made without water, which relies on the juice from lots of skinned fresh tomatoes. It is usually served garnished with Serrano ham, which I like to crisp up to add texture, and chopped hard-boiled eggs, but I also serve it from time to time topped with some flaked, good-quality, olive-oil-preserved tuna (see page 158) in place of the crisp-fried ham. *Salmorejo* is typically found in Cordoba, but is enjoyed throughout Spain.

Serves 6–8

12 oz slightly stale country-style bread, crusts removed (to give 8 oz crustless white bread)

2¼ lb ripe and juicy vine-ripened tomatoes, skinned

3 garlic cloves, crushed

pinch of sugar (only if your tomatoes lack sweetness)

²/₃ cup good-quality olive oil, plus 1 tablespoon, and extra to serve

2 tablespoons sherry vinegar

2 large free-range eggs

6–8 thin slices of Serrano ham

½ cup good-quality green or black pitted olives, quartered lengthwise

sea salt

Break the bread into a bowl and sprinkle with 1 cup water. Leave to soak for at least 30 minutes. Meanwhile, quarter the tomatoes, and scoop out the seeds into a sieve set over another bowl. Roughly chop the flesh and rub the juices from the seeds through the sieve. Discard the seeds.

Put the tomato flesh and juices into a blender with the garlic and sugar (if using), and blend until smooth. Squeeze as much water as you can from the bread, add the bread to the blender, and blend once more, then, with the motor still running, gradually pour in ²/₃ cup of the oil, the vinegar, and 1½ teaspoons salt. The mixture should be thick, but not stiff. Pour into a bowl, cover, and chill for at least 2 hours. Chill 4 small soup bowls.

Shortly before serving, lower the eggs into a pan of boiling water, and cook for 9 minutes. Drain, cover with cold water, and, when they are cold, peel off the shells and chop both eggs roughly into small pieces.

Heat the remaining tablespoon of oil in a large frying pan over medium heat. Add 2 slices of ham side by side, and fry for about 30 seconds on each side, until crisp and lightly golden. Lift onto paper towels to drain and cool. Repeat with the remaining ham. Once it is cold, crumble into small pieces.

To serve, spoon the soup into the chilled bowls and garnish with the chopped egg, crisp ham, and olives. Drizzle over a little more olive oil, and serve immediately while it is still cold.

Shrimp baked in salt with anise and fennel herb mayonnaise

Whenever I visit Huelva, on the south Andalucian coast, I always go to a restaurant called Casa Machaquito in Islantilla and have *langostinos* (jumbo shrimp) baked in salt. Those shrimp are caught in the area and can cost as much as $110 a pound! Their flavor is indescribable—they are so good and taste so sweet. The casing of salt seals in the flavor of the shrimp and enhances the taste of the sea, without making them at all salty. I like to add a few fennel seeds to the salt mixture to give extra flavor, and then echo this in some mayonnaise, flavored with anise liqueur and fennel herb, for dipping. A delicious dish for a special occasion.

Serves 4

1 large egg white

5½ lb coarse rock salt

4 tablespoons fennel seeds, lightly crushed

20 raw unpeeled jumbo shrimp (as large as you can find, or as expensive as you can afford)

To serve

⅔ cup Olive Oil Mayonnaise (see page 227), made without the mustard

1½ teaspoons Pernod or other anise liqueur

1 tablespoon chopped fennel herb

Preheat the oven to 400°F. Put the egg white into a bowl, and whisk until it forms soft peaks. Stir in the rock salt and crushed fennel seeds, then spread half of the mixture in a ½-inch even layer over the base of a large roasting pan.

Lay the jumbo shrimp side by side on top of the salt, and cover with the remaining mixture, ensuring that the shrimp are completely covered, and there are no gaps. Bake in the oven for 8 minutes, by which time the shrimp should be cooked through. However, if they are very thick and meaty, give them an extra couple of minutes.

Remove the pan from the oven, and break open the now hard salt crust. Lift the shrimp onto a serving plate. Stir the anise liqueur and fennel herb into the mayonnaise, and serve with the shrimp.

Tuna confit with potato salad, roasted red peppers, and capers

The tuna from Huelva is fished in the centuries-old way called *almadraba*, where the fishermen use stretched maze-like nets to catch it. Always use a nice thick piece of tuna for the confit, so it doesn't cook through too quickly, and become dry and tough. And I like to use lemon in this salad and the confit to add an acidity to cut through the tuna. This recipe makes more tuna confit than is needed, so store any left over in the fridge, covered in olive oil, for up to 30 days.

Serves 6–8

1 x 18 oz piece tuna loin, cut 2 inches thick

approx. 2½ cups good quality olive oil

3 fresh bay leaves

3 strips of pared lemon zest

2 large thyme sprigs

½ teaspoon black peppercorns

For the salad

2¼ lb small waxy new potatoes

1 large red bell pepper

2 scallions, thinly sliced

2 tablespoons small capers, rinsed and
   drained, plus extra to garnish

For the dressing

6 tablespoons extra-virgin olive oil

2 tablespoons lemon juice

sea salt and freshly ground black pepper

The day before you wish to serve this dish, make the tuna confit. Rub the tuna all over with 2 teaspoons sea salt and set aside for 1 hour. Put the oil, bay leaves, lemon zest, thyme, and peppercorns into a pan in which the tuna will fit quite snugly, and heat it to 140°F. Leave over low heat, trying to maintain this temperature, for 20 minutes. Then remove and set aside.

Add the piece of salted tuna to the oil and bring the temperature of the oil up to 185°F. Leave at this temperature for 10 minutes, then remove from the heat and allow to cool, by which time the tuna should be perfectly cooked through. Transfer to a glass bowl or plastic box, cover and refrigerate until needed.

For the salad, cook the potatoes in salted water for 15–20 minutes until tender. Meanwhile, place the red pepper under a hot broiler and cook for 20 minutes, turning it occasionally, until the skin is quite black. Remove from the broiler, and drop into a plastic bag to cool, then remove and discard the stalk, seeds, and skin, and cut the flesh into thin strips.

Drain the potatoes and break them into small chunks into a bowl. For the dressing, whisk the olive oil and lemon juice together with ½ teaspoon sea salt and some black pepper. While the potatoes are still warm, stir in the dressing, and leave them to cool. Then stir in the scallions, capers, and a little more seasoning to taste.

Remove the tuna from the oil, and flake 5 oz of it into small chunks. Spoon the potato salad onto a shallow serving plate and scatter over the roasted red pepper strips and the flaked tuna. Scatter over a few more capers, drizzle with a little more oil and sprinkle with a little more sea salt, then serve.

Seared tuna steak with salsa verde on grilled potatoes

The last time I was cooking for my great friend and photographer Emma Lee, I overcooked the tuna—I was chatting too much and forgot to check it, but she was happy and satisfied when I cooked this dish for her for this book! Adding olives to a salsa verde gives extra flavor and an oiliness, which complements the tuna. This recipe makes a generous amount of salsa verde, but it is also wonderful served with grilled steaks.

Serves 4

18 oz small, evenly sized waxy new potatoes

1 tablespoon olive oil, plus extra for brushing

sea salt and freshly ground black pepper

4 x 7 oz tuna steaks, cut 1¼ inches thick

For the salsa verde

⅓ cup each of flat-leaf parsley leaves, mint leaves and basil leaves

1 garlic clove, thinly sliced

2 tablespoons salted capers, rinsed well, drained, and dried

½ cup good-quality pitted green olives

4 anchovy fillets in oil

finely grated zest of ¼ small lemon

1 teaspoon Dijon mustard

1½ tablespoons lemon juice

8 tablespoons extra-virgin olive oil

Cut the potatoes into ¼-inch-thick slices. Put them into a pan of salted cold water, bring to a boil, and simmer for 5 minutes, or until they are only just tender when pierced with the tip of a knife. Drain well, leave the steam to die down, then toss them with 1 tablespoon olive oil, and some salt and pepper.

For the salsa verde, drop the herbs into boiling water, leave for 5 seconds, then drain and refresh under cold water. Squeeze out all the excess water, then put onto a chopping board with the sliced garlic, capers, olives, and anchovies, and finely chop everything together. Scoop the mixture into a bowl, and stir in the lemon zest, mustard, lemon juice, olive oil, and some freshly ground black pepper.

Heat a cast-iron grill pan over high heat, then reduce the heat to medium. Add half the sliced potatoes in one layer, and grill for about 3 minutes on each side until golden. Transfer to a baking sheet, sprinkle with a little more salt, and keep hot in a low oven while you cook the remainder. Add them to the baking sheet and keep hot.

Brush the tuna steaks with oil and season. Return the cast-iron grill pan to high heat, and when it is smoking hot, reduce the heat to medium-high. Place the steaks side-by-side on the grill pan and cook for 1–1½ minutes on each side until nicely marked on the outside, but still rare in the center.

As you turn the tuna steaks over, divide the potatoes between 4 warmed plates. Put the tuna on top, spoon over some of the salsa verde, and serve.

Salad of pears, mojama, arugula, pine nuts, and olive oil

Mojama is filleted salt-cured and air-dried tuna from Cadiz. Tuna loins are salted for 2 days, then the salt is removed, and the tuna is laid out to dry in the sun for 15–20 days. Everyone knows the classic combination of pears, nuts and blue cheese —here the salty mojama works like the blue cheese to create a pleasing balance of tastes and textures.

Serves 4

2 ripe but firm dessert pears

2 cups wild arugula

3 oz mojama (salt-cured and air-dried tuna), thinly shaved

⅓ cup pine nuts, toasted

For the dressing

3 tablespoons extra-virgin olive oil

1 tablespoon lemon juice

2 teaspoons honey

1 teaspoon Dijon mustard

sea salt and freshly ground black pepper

To make the dressing, whisk together the olive oil, lemon juice, honey, mustard, and some salt and pepper.

Quarter, core and peel the pears, then cut them lengthwise into thin wedges. Put them into a bowl, and toss them with 1 tablespoon of the dressing. Toss the arugula in another bowl with another tablespoon of the dressing.

Arrange the pears and arugula on 4 plates and drizzle over the remaining dressing. Scatter over the mojama shavings and pine nuts, and serve.

Deep-fried red mullet with green olive mayonnaise and dressed green leaves

Every time I go to southern Spain I gorge on fried fish, and the red mullet from this area of the Mediterranean is exceptional. The Andalusians love to deep-fry fish, simply dusted in fine bread crumbs and flour. If you want more crispiness, you can use chickpea flour. I like to put green olives in mayonnaise—I use the Andalusian Manzanilla olives, but if you can't get hold of them use good-quality, large, juicy, fresh green olives. This is my brother Antonio's favorite recipe.

Serves 4

olive or sunflower oil, for deep-frying

4 x 8–10 oz whole red mullet or snapper, cleaned and trimmed

flour, for coating

sea salt and freshly ground black pepper

For the green olive mayonnaise

½ quantity Olive Oil Mayonnaise (see page 227)

1 teaspoon sherry vinegar

finely grated zest of ½ small lemon

1 tablespoon finely chopped shallot

2 teaspoons finely chopped green olives

2 teaspoons finely chopped gherkins

2 teaspoons capers, rinsed, drained and chopped

2 teaspoons chopped flat-leaf parsley

For the dressed green leaves

1 soft-leaved lettuce, broken into leaves

1 large scallion, thinly sliced

3 tablespoons extra-virgin olive oil

1 tablespoon lemon juice

pinch of superfine sugar

Mix all the ingredients for the green olive mayonnaise with some salt to taste, and spoon it into a small serving bowl.

Toss the lettuce leaves in a bowl with the scallion. Make a dressing by whisking the extra-virgin olive oil with the lemon juice, sugar, and seasoning, and set aside.

Heat some oil for deep-frying to 350°F and preheat the oven to 225°F. Season the fish inside and out, coat generously with flour, and shake off the excess. Deep-fry one at a time for 3 minutes until cooked through. Lift onto paper towels, and keep hot in the oven while you cook the other fish.

Toss the lettuce leaves with the dressing and serve with the fried fish and the green olive mayonnaise.

Whole sea bass baked on anchovy and garlic potatoes

You can make this recipe with any whole large fish. Red snapper is especially good if you can't easily get hold of sea bass. This is a great celebratory dish for a special occasion—I love to make this dish for all my friends.

Serves 6

3¼ lb large waxy new potatoes

4 large garlic cloves, thinly sliced

8 anchovy fillets in olive oil, drained
and sliced

1 whole (approx. 3¾ lb) sea bass or red
snapper, cleaned and scaled

1 lemon, thinly sliced

3 bay leaves

3 lemon leaves (if available)

sea salt and freshly ground black pepper

For the dressing

8 tablespoons extra-virgin olive oil

3 tablespoons lemon juice

3 tablespoons chopped fresh oregano
or marjoram

Preheat the oven to 400°F. Make the dressing by whisking the olive oil with the lemon juice, 1½ teaspoons salt, and some pepper, then stir in the chopped oregano or marjoram. Cut the potatoes into ⅜-inch-thick slices, and put them into a large roasting pan in which the fish fits either lengthwise or diagonally. Add 6 tablespoons of the dressing, the sliced garlic, and anchovies and toss well together. Spread out in an even layer, and roast in the oven for 30–35 minutes.

Slash the flesh of the fish 5–6 times on each side. Season the cavity with salt and pepper, then stuff it with the lemon slices, bay leaves, and lemon leaves (if using). Remove the pan of potatoes from the oven, and release the slices from the bottom of the pan if they have stuck. Brush the outside of the fish with a little of the remaining dressing, and season with salt and pepper. Put it on top of the potatoes, and pour any remaining dressing into the cavity of the fish. Return the roasting pan to the oven, and roast for another 35 minutes, until the fish is cooked through, and the potatoes are tender. Serve hot.

Spicy lamb albondigas

It is believed that the concept of *albondigas* (meatballs) came from the Moors, with their dish of *kofte*. In Spain, lamb is not often used for meatballs, but I love the combination of lamb with these spices and ham. In my family, we always eat meatballs with fried potatoes, but you can serve them with plain rice.

Serves 4

2 slices white bread, crusts removed

3 tablespoons milk

4 oz Serrano ham, thinly sliced

1¼ lb ground lamb

2 garlic cloves, crushed

1½ teaspoons freshly ground cumin seeds

1½ teaspoons freshly ground coriander seeds

¾ teaspoon hot paprika

2 tablespoons chopped flat-leaf parsley

4 tablespoons olive oil, for frying

sea salt and freshly ground black pepper

For the sauce

3 tablespoons olive oil

1 heaping cup shallots, finely chopped

3 garlic cloves, crushed

½ teaspoon crushed dried red pepper flakes

28 oz skinned, chopped vine-ripened tomatoes, fresh or canned

7 fl oz good-quality Fino sherry

7 fl oz homemade chicken stock

2 bay leaves

To serve

chopped flat-leaf parsley

extra-virgin olive oil

1 quantity *patatas fritas* (see page 117)

Soak the bread in the milk for 5 minutes. Put the Serrano ham into a food processor, and chop finely, using the pulse button. Squeeze the excess milk from the bread, and put it into a bowl with the chopped ham, ground lamb, garlic, spices, parsley, ¼ teaspoon of salt, and some pepper. Mix well together, then shape into about 32 meatballs.

Heat half the olive oil in a large frying pan over medium-high heat. Add some of the meatballs, and fry until golden brown all over. Remove them from the pan. Continue to fry the meatballs in batches, adding the remaining olive oil as necessary, until they are all browned.

For the sauce, heat the olive oil in a wide deep frying pan. Add the shallots, garlic, and red pepper flakes and fry gently for 8–10 minutes until soft, but not browned. Add the tomatoes, sherry, stock, bay leaves, and some salt and black pepper, and simmer very gently, stirring occasionally, for 1 hour, until it has reduced and thickened.

Add the meatballs and simmer gently for 5 minutes, or until heated through. Remove and discard the bay leaves. Spoon the meatballs onto a plate, scatter with a little chopped parsley, and drizzle with a little extra-virgin olive oil. Serve with *patatas fritas*.

Deep-fried chicken wings al ajillo

These chicken wings are great for a party and go really well with sherry—especially *Amontillado abocado*. They are served in all the tapas bars in Andalusia. Normally you don't use too much chili pepper, but I love to add a real kick of heat to my *ajillo* (garlic dressing).

Serves 6

24 large, meaty, free-range (cage-free)
  chicken wings

olive or sunflower oil, for deep-frying

For the ajillo

6 fat garlic cloves

6 tablespoons extra-virgin olive oil

1½ teaspoons crushed dried red pepper
  flakes

1½ teaspoons sweet paprika

4 teaspoons sherry vinegar

sea salt

Cut off the pointy tips from each chicken wing and discard. Dry the wings well on paper towels. Heat the oil for deep-frying to 350°F. Add a quarter of the chicken wings and cook for 6–7 minutes, until cooked through, crisp, and golden.

Meanwhile, for the dressing, put the garlic cloves on a board, sprinkle with some salt, and crush them into a smooth paste with the blade of a large knife. Put the extra-virgin olive oil and the garlic in a small pan, and place it over medium-low heat. As soon as the garlic begins to sizzle, add the red pepper flakes and cook very gently for about 2 minutes, until the garlic is very lightly golden. Stir in the paprika and sherry vinegar, and remove from the heat.

As soon as the first batch of chicken wings is cooked, drain them briefly on paper towels, transfer them to a serving bowl, and drizzle with some of the warm garlic and chili dressing. Toss well together, sprinkle with a little sea salt and serve hot. Repeat with the remaining wings.

Pan-fried duck with a sherry, raisin, and pine nut sauce

As Jerez is in the south of Spain, I have used sherry for this dish. In my cooking, I use Oloroso sherry in the same way as red wine, but Oloroso gives extra flavor because of the yeast in the sherry.

Serves 4

$1/3$ cup raisins
$1\frac{1}{4}$ cups Oloroso sherry
4 x 6–7 oz duck breasts
2 tablespoons superfine sugar
1 tablespoon red wine vinegar
$3/4$ teaspoon arrowroot
2 teaspoons sherry vinegar
$1/4$ cup pine nuts, toasted
sea salt and freshly ground black pepper
watercress sprigs, to garnish

Soak the raisins in the sherry overnight. Remove the duck breasts from their packaging, put them on a plate, cover them loosely with a sheet of parchment paper, and leave them somewhere cool overnight. This will help to dry out the skin, and make it extra crispy.

The next day, put the sugar into a small pan with 1 tablespoon cold water and leave over low heat until the sugar has completely dissolved. Increase the heat and boil vigorously until the syrup turns into a deep amber-colored caramel. Remove the pan from the heat, and add the vinegar (take care as it will bubble quite energetically). Return the pan to the heat, add the soaked raisins and the sherry, and leave to simmer gently for 20 minutes. Mix the arrowroot with 2 tablespoons water, stir into the sauce, and simmer for 1 minute. Season to taste, and keep warm over low heat.

Lightly score the skin of each duck breast into a diamond pattern, taking care not to cut down into the flesh. Season the meat with salt and pepper and the skin with just salt.

Heat a dry, heavy-based frying pan over high heat. Add the duck breasts, skin-side down, reduce the heat to medium, and cook them for 3–4 minutes until the skin is crisp and golden brown. Turn the breasts over and cook them for 5 minutes if you like them pink, or slightly longer if you like them a little more cooked.

Remove the breasts from the pan onto a board and leave them to rest for 5 minutes. Then slice each one diagonally into long thin slices, and transfer onto 4 warmed plates. Stir the sherry vinegar and toasted pine nuts into the sauce, and spoon it over the duck. Garnish with the watercress, and serve.

Oxtail with cinnamon, red wine, sherry vinegar, and dried plums

Oxtail are often eaten in southern Spain, and this is my adaptation of the classical oxtail stews. When you cook the prunes with vinegar, they caramelize to give a wonderful flavor.

Serves 4–6

4½ lb oxtail, cut into chunks

flour, for coating

5 tablespoons olive oil

5 tablespoons sherry vinegar

2 medium onions, chopped

1 small head of garlic, separated into cloves
   and peeled

2 inch cinnamon stick

½ teaspoon ground allspice

7 oz skinned, chopped tomatoes,
   fresh or canned

2 cups red wine, such as Tempranillo

2 cups beef stock

4 strips of pared orange zest

1 bouquet garni (parsley stalks, bay leaves,
   and thyme)

1–2 tablespoons honey

9 oz dried plums (not the no-soak ones)

7 fl oz port wine

14 oz small shallots or baby onions, peeled

11 oz carrots, cut into small chunks

2 celery stalks, sliced

sea salt and freshly ground black pepper

chopped parsley, to garnish

Olive Oil Mashed Potatoes or *patatas fritas*,
   to serve (see pages 33 and 117)

Season the oxtail well with salt and pepper, then coat the pieces in flour, and knock off the excess. Heat 3 tablespoons of the oil in a large, flameproof casserole, add half the oxtail pieces, and fry until well-browned all over. Do this slowly so that you get a really rich brown color, and lots of flavor without it burning on the base of the casserole. Lift the first batch into a bowl, and repeat with the remainder.

Pour the excess oil from the casserole into a small bowl. Add the sherry vinegar to the pan, and scrape the base with a wooden spoon as the liquid boils to release all the caramelized bits. Add to the bowl with the oxtail.

Return 3 tablespoons of the reserved oil to the casserole with the onions and garlic cloves, cover, and cook, stirring occasionally, for 10–12 minutes, until soft and golden brown. Stir in the cinnamon, allspice, and the tomatoes, and fry for 2–3 minutes more. Add the red wine, beef stock, orange zest, bouquet garni, and 1 tablespoon of the honey. Return the oxtail, all the juices from the bowl, and some seasoning to the casserole, bring to a boil, cover, and simmer gently for 2½ hours, turning the pieces of oxtail over occasionally, until just tender, but not falling apart.

Remove the casserole from the heat, and discard the cinnamon stick and herbs, and leave to cool, then chill overnight. Put the dried plums into a small bowl with the port, and leave them to soak overnight.

The next day, remove the fat from the surface of the casserole and bring it back to a simmer over low heat. Heat the remaining olive oil in a large pan. Add the shallots or baby onions, cover, and fry gently until golden brown all over. Add the carrots and celery, and fry for another 5 minutes until lightly browned. Stir into the oxtail with the dried plums and port. Re-cover and simmer for 30 minutes until the vegetables are tender. Stir in a little more honey if you wish, and adjust the seasoning to taste. Sprinkle with the chopped parsley, and serve with olive oil mashed potatoes or *patatas fritas*.

Flamenquin

These are among one of the most popular tapas in Andalusia and the literal translation is "small flamenco dancer." They are fried veal, ham, and cheese rolls.

Serves 4

4 x 5 oz veal or pork scallops

8 thin slices of Serrano ham

3½ oz *Queso de Grazalema* or Gruyère cheese, cut into 8 long sticks about ½-inch thick

olive oil, for shallow-frying

flour, for coating

2 extra large eggs, beaten

1¼ cups white breadcrumbs

For the tomato sauce

scant ½ cup olive oil

1 large onion, finely chopped

4 garlic cloves, finely chopped

14 oz skinned, chopped tomatoes, fresh or canned

⅔ cup chicken stock

3 fresh bay leaves

1 tablespoon chopped oregano or marjoram

2 tablespoons small capers, rinsed and drained

¼ cup pitted black olives, cut lengthways into strips

sugar, sea salt, and freshly ground black pepper

For the tomato sauce, heat the olive oil in a medium pan. Add the onion and garlic, cover, and cook gently for 10 minutes until very soft and lightly golden. Add the tomatoes, chicken stock, and bay leaves and simmer, uncovered, for 30–40 minutes, stirring occasionally, until the sauce has reduced, and thickened to a good consistency.

Meanwhile, prepare the scallops. Place each one in turn between 2 sheets of plastic wrap and gently flatten with a rolling pin until uniformly thin. Cut each one in half, and season lightly on both sides. Cover the pieces with a slice of Serrano ham. Lay the lengths of cheese across one short edge of each scallop, neatly roll them up, and secure in place with a wooden cocktail stick.

Remove the bay leaves from the tomato sauce and discard, spoon half of it into a mini food processor and blend until smooth. Stir it back into the pan with the oregano or marjoram, capers, olives, and some sugar, salt, and pepper to taste, and leave to simmer for another 5 minutes. Keep hot.

Meanwhile, pour 1 inch of olive oil in a deep sauté pan or wide-based saucepan, and heat to 325°F. Dip the rolls first into the flour, then the beaten eggs, and finally the breadcrumbs, and ensure they are well coated. Add them to the hot oil, and fry for 5–7 minutes, turning them over frequently, until they are golden brown and cooked through. Drain briefly on paper towels, carefully remove the cocktail sticks, and serve with the tomato sauce.

Hanging poached peaches with lemon and olive oil ice cream

In Spain they wrap the peaches in tissue paper when they are hanging on the tree, so I love the idea of "hanging poached peaches." You can make the peaches and keep them preserved in bottles. My mom used to do this so we could eat peaches throughout the year. For the ice cream, use the best fruity Arbequina olive oil that you can find—it is perfectly mild and fruity.

Serves 4

4 large, ripe peaches

1 vanilla bean

2 cups sweet white wine, such as
    Moscatel de Chipiona

2 tablespoons honey

For the ice cream

7 fl oz whole milk

5 extra large egg yolks

½ cup superfine sugar

1¼ cups heavy cream

finely grated zest of 1 lemon

⅔ cup fruity Arbequina olive oil

For the ice cream, bring the milk to a boil in a medium pan. Meanwhile, whisk the egg yolks with the sugar until pale and thick. Gradually whisk in the hot milk, strain the mixture back into the pan, and cook over gentle heat, stirring constantly, until the mixture coats the back of a wooden spoon. Remove from the heat, leave to cool, then stir in the cream, lemon zest, and olive oil and refrigerate overnight.

The next day, churn the ice cream mixture in an ice cream machine. Alternatively, pour it into a shallow container, and freeze until almost solid. Scrape into the bowl of a food processor, and blend briefly until smooth, then return to the container, and freeze once again. Repeat this 2–3 times more, until the mixture is very smooth. Return to the freezer for 6 hours until firm, or until needed.

Put the peaches into a heatproof bowl. Fill another bowl with ice water. Cover the peaches with boiling water and leave for 30 seconds, then remove and drop into the ice water. The skins should now peel away easily.

Slice the vanilla bean in half lengthwise and scrape out the seeds with the tip of a knife. Put the bean and seeds into a pan (choose one in which the peaches will fit snugly in a single layer) with the sweet wine and honey, and heat gently until the honey has dissolved. Add the peaches, bring to a simmer, cover, and cook very gently for 15 minutes, carefully turning them over occasionally with a wooden spoon, until they are just tender and can be pierced easily through to the pit with a toothpick.

When the peaches are cooked, gently transfer them and the vanilla bean to a bowl. Return the syrup to the heat, and boil rapidly until reduced to just under 1 cup. Leave to cool, then pour back over the peaches, and chill until needed. Serve with the lemon and olive oil ice cream.

Flan de naranja

I remember coming home when I was a child, and going to the fridge, taking out a whole flan (baked caramel custard), and eating it all. In Spain we make one large flan rather than small individual ones. I think this dish is even better with the addition of orange zest; it is now top of my list of desserts, and that's why I serve it in my restaurant, Pizarro.

Serves 8–10

heaping ¾ cup superfine sugar, plus
  6 tablespoons

1 quart whole milk

finely grated zest of 8 large oranges

6 extra large eggs, plus 6 extra large
  egg yolks

Preheat the oven to 325°F. Place a shallow 1½ quart oval baking dish into the oven to warm. Put the heaping ¾ cup of the sugar into a medium pan with a scant ½ cup cold water and leave it over low heat until the sugar has dissolved, then increase the heat, and boil rapidly until the mixture has turned into a dark amber caramel. Remove from the heat, and quickly pour the caramel into the warmed dish, tilting it backwards and forwards to cover the base and ½ inch up the sides in a thin, even layer. Set aside.

Put the milk, remaining sugar, and orange zest into a clean pan, and bring to simmering point. Remove from the heat and set aside for 30 minutes.

Put the eggs and egg yolks into a bowl and whisk together lightly. Strain the orange-infused milk, and whisk it into the eggs. Pour the mixture into the baking dish and put it into a small roasting pan. Pour hot (but not boiling) water into the pan until it comes halfway up the sides of the dish. Bake in the oven for 45–50 minutes, or until the mixture has just set, but still has a slight wobble in the center. It will continue to firm up as it cools. Remove the dish from the roasting pan, and leave to cool, then chill for 6 hours or overnight.

To serve, run a round-bladed knife around the edge of the dish, and invert onto a serving dish. Pour over the caramel juices, and serve.

Strawberries in sherry vinegar with goat cheese parfait and praline

People often serve strawberries with balsamic vinegar, but sherry vinegar works just as well. The goat cheese parfait adds a creaminess and the praline a sweet crunchiness.

Serves 8

1 lb small strawberries
4 teaspoons superfine sugar
1 tablespoon sweet Pedro Ximenez sherry vinegar

For the goat cheese parfait

7 fl oz whole milk
5 extra large egg yolks
¼ cup superfine sugar
scant ½ cup heavy cream
5 oz soft, rindless goat cheese
3 tablespoons liquid glucose
scant ½ cup whole-milk plain yogurt

For the praline

¼ cup superfine sugar
6 tablespoons slivered almonds, toasted

For the goat cheese parfait, bring the milk slowly to a boil in a medium nonstick pan. Meanwhile, beat together the egg yolks and sugar in a mixing bowl until pale and creamy. Whisk the hot milk into the egg yolks, return the mixture to the pan, and stir over low heat until the mixture thickens, and coats the back of a wooden spoon. Pour into a bowl and leave to cool. Stir in the cream, and chill overnight.

The next day, put the goat cheese into a bowl with the liquid glucose and yogurt, and beat until smooth, then gradually beat in the chilled custard. Churn the mixture in an ice cream machine. Alternatively, pour it into a shallow container and freeze until almost solid. Scrape into the bowl of a food processor, and blend briefly until smooth, then return to the container and freeze once again. Repeat this 2–3 times more, until the mixture is very smooth. Spoon the mixture evenly into 8 dariole molds or small (½ cup) ramekins, cover with plastic wrap, and freeze for 4 hours until firm or until needed.

For the praline, line a baking sheet with parchment paper. Put the superfine sugar in a small pan with 2 tablespoons water. Leave over low heat until the sugar has completely dissolved, then boil rapidly until it has turned into a brick-red caramel. Remove from the heat, quickly stir in the slivered almonds, pour onto the paper-lined baking sheet, and spread out into a thin layer. Allow to become cold, then transfer to a mini food processor, and blend briefly until finely crushed.

Shortly before serving, halve the strawberries into a bowl, and stir in the sugar and sherry vinegar. Leave to stand for 5 minutes. Unmold the goat cheese parfaits onto plates, and sprinkle with praline. Spoon some of the strawberries alongside, and serve.

You can store any leftover praline in an airtight container—it's lovely sprinkled over vanilla ice cream.

Candied orange torrijas with bitter orange caramel

Torrijas is the Spanish form of British Eggy Bread, French Pain Perdu or American French Toast—fresh bread, soaked in a rich and creamy egg custard and then pan-fried in butter until crisp and golden. The twist of sweet candied orange and bitter orange caramel takes this to a more sophisticated level.

Serves 4

For the torrijas

16 small, medium-thick slices of white bread

1½ sticks butter, softened

¾ cup good-quality chopped candied orange peel

3 large eggs

½ cup heavy cream, plus extra to serve

½ cup whole milk

few drops of vanilla extract

¼ cup superfine sugar, for sprinkling

For the bitter orange caramel

6 tablespoons superfine sugar

2 tablespoons cold water

1 tablespoon orange liqueur

2½ tablespoons freshly squeezed orange juice, strained

For the bitter orange caramel, put the sugar and water into a small pan, and leave over low heat until the sugar has completely dissolved. Then increase the heat, and leave the syrup to boil rapidly until it has turned into a brick-red caramel. Stand back and add the orange liqueur (it will splutter quite ferociously), then plunge the base of the pan into cold water to stop it cooking any further. Return the pan to low heat, add the orange juice, and leave until all the caramel has dissolved once more. Pour the mixture into a bowl, or small glass jar and leave to go cold. This can be made ahead of time if you wish.

For the *torrijas*, cut a 2¾-inch disk from each slice of bread, and spread with a little of the butter. Spoon the candied orange peel into the buttered center of 8 of the disks, cover with the remaining 8 disks, buttered side down, and press well together around the edges to seal.

Beat together the eggs, cream, milk, and vanilla extract in a shallow dish. Gently melt the remaining butter in a small pan, and pour off the clear butter into a small bowl, leaving behind the milky-white liquid at the bottom of the pan.

Pour some of the clarified butter into a large nonstick frying pan, and place it over medium heat. Dip the *torrijas* into the egg mixture one at a time, leave for a few seconds, then turn over, making sure they are evenly coated, and well soaked in the mixture. Add some of them to the frying pan, and fry for 2 minutes on each side until crisp and golden. Drain briefly on paper towels and keep hot. Repeat with the remaining butter and *torrijas*. Serve hot, sprinkled with superfine sugar, and drizzled with a little heavy cream, and some of the bitter orange caramel.

Almond, raisin, and lemon cake

This is a deliciously moist cake, studded with raisins. The recipe was inspired by the excellent Malaga raisins of the region. It can be served warm as a dessert, or is excellent cold with strong coffee. It keeps well for a few days in an airtight container.

Serves 10–12

1½ sticks softened butter, plus extra
for greasing

scant ½ cup all-purpose flour, plus extra
for dusting

heaping ½ cup good-quality raisins

heaping 1 cup superfine sugar, plus extra
for dusting

finely grated zest of 1 lemon

4 extra large eggs

heaping 1 cup ground almonds

2 tablespoons lemon juice

Preheat the oven to 350°F. Grease an 8-inch loose-based, 2-inch deep cake pan and base-line with parchment paper. Grease the paper and then dust the pan with a little flour. Put the raisins into a food processor with 2 teaspoons of the flour and whizz briefly, using the pulse button until they are finely chopped. Beat the butter and sugar together in a mixing bowl until very pale and fluffy. Add the lemon zest. Beat in the eggs, one at a time, adding a little of the flour with the last egg. Fold in the remaining flour, the ground almonds, raisins, and lemon juice. Spoon the mixture evenly into the prepared pan and bake for 45 minutes, loosely covering the top with a sheet of foil after 30 minutes to stop it browning too much. Run a knife around the outside of the cake and turn it out onto a cooling rack covered with a sheet of paper towels. Remove the base of the tin and the lining paper, cover with a second cooling rack, and turn it back over again. Dust with superfine sugar and leave to cool.

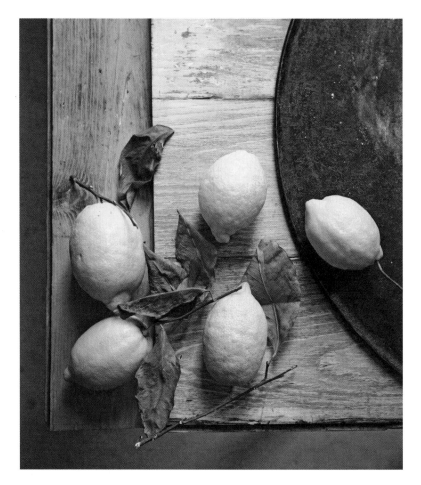

Payoyo with Seville orange chutney

Payoyo is a very rich, hard sheep's cheese from Cadiz, from the beautiful area of Grazalema. If you can't get it, use the well-known Manchego. Seville oranges are normally used to make marmalade, but this chutney is stunning, and goes so well with this local cheese.

Serves 8

18 oz Payoyo cheese, thinly sliced

For the Seville orange chutney

$^3/_8$ cup raisins

4 tablespoons sherry vinegar

4 tablespoons Oloroso sherry

2 tablespoons butter

1 tablespoon olive oil

9 oz pickling onions (or small shallots), peeled

$^1/_3$ cup shallots, finely chopped

juice of 3 Seville oranges (about 9 tablespoons) or 6 tablespoons orange juice and 3 tablespoons lemon juice

5 tablespoons coarse-cut Seville orange marmalade

8 cloves

pinch of ground allspice

fine sea salt

Put the raisins, sherry vinegar, and sherry into a small pan, and bring to a simmer over low heat. Remove from the heat, and leave the raisins to plump up for 30 minutes.

Heat the butter and olive oil in a medium pan, add the pickling onions, cover, and cook gently for 10 minutes, shaking the pan occasionally, until they are golden brown, and starting to soften.

Stir in the chopped shallots, re-cover and cook gently for another 5 minutes until soft. Add the raisin and sherry vinegar mixture, re-cover the pan, and continue to cook gently for 10 minutes, until the pickling onions are quite soft. Add the Seville orange (or orange and lemon) juice, the marmalade, cloves, allspice, and a good pinch of salt, partially cover the pan, and simmer, stirring occasionally, for 20 minutes, or until the onions have just collapsed, and the mixture has reduced and thickened. Allow to cool, then serve with thin slices of Payoyo cheese.

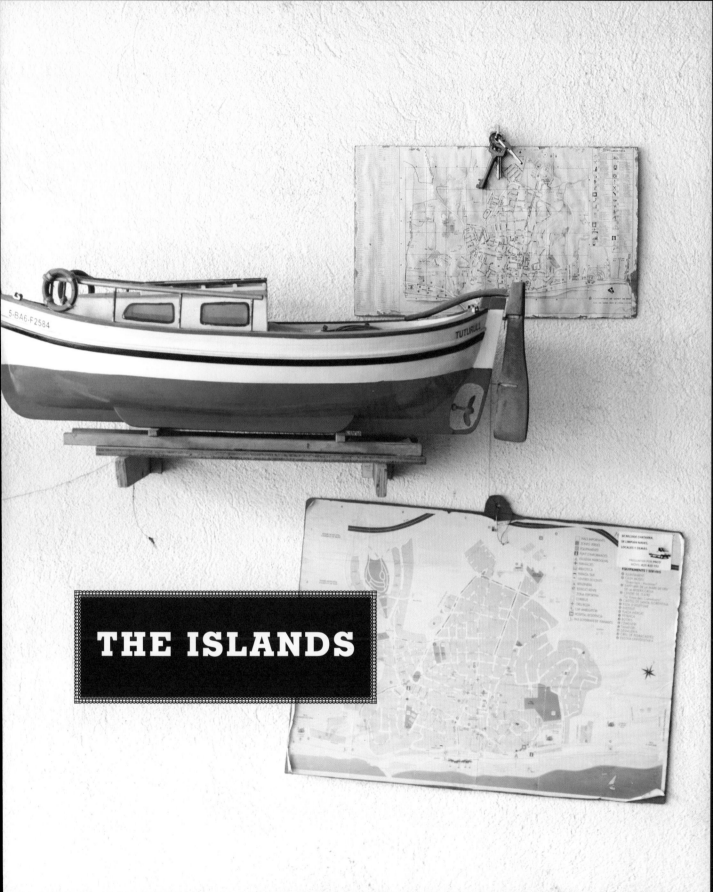

THE ISLANDS

THE ISLANDS: INTRODUCTION

The Canary and the Balearic islands are much more than tourist destinations with big hotels and all-day and all-night clubs. Away from the hot spots, there are also incredible areas of tranquility and amazing beaches. And the great gastronomic culture of these islands is protected by the water that surrounds them. Even though they are hundreds of miles apart, the food of these two sets of islands are similar in their simplicity, freshness and strong flavors.

I have to admit that my first visit to the Canaries was for the Carnival of Tenerife, which is one of the things that you have to do once in your life when you are young! The carnival spirit was imported for sure, from the New World, since the ports of the Canary Islands were very important stopping places during the age of seafaring discoverers and conquerors. The links are evident from the islanders' colorful cultural dress, as well as from the diversity of tropical fruits that are now cultivated here: mangoes, avocados, pineapples, and bananas. I can still recall the incredible contrast of the thronging beach resorts and high-rise hotels with the jungle-like banana plantations that are so huge you could easily become lost.

The Canary Islands are not just known for their tropical fruits, but for the great variety of stews—my favorite is the Canary stew (on page 197), the *mojos* or cold sauces made with a base of oil and vinegar, and served as a dressing to accompany fish or meat, and one of the islands' star dishes: "wrinkled potatoes"—*patatas arrugas* (page 191), which have become a must-have snack at almost all of my parties at home.

My earliest gastronomic memory of the Balearic Islands is from Menorca, the most easterly of the group. It was a delicious lobster stew, *caldereta de langosta*—a specialty of the island, which encapsulates the healthy, simple style of Mediterranean cuisine. As the locals will tell you, lobsters from the warm shallow waters around Menorca have an exquisitely delicate and sweet flavor. One of Spain's few cheeses made from cow's milk is made on Menorca, called Mahón. It is slightly sharp, with a salty tang, and it's one of my favorite cheeses.

Pork is a very important ingredient in Balearic cuisine. For me the most notable speciality is the *sobrasada*, a soft, spicy sausage that I love to eat with toast and a drizzle of honey. On Mallorca you will often see people returning home with a round box that contains an *ensaïmada*, which is a type of yeast-based pastry made with pork lard, which is fashioned into a coil before being baked. You must try both of these things if you are lucky enough to be in the Balearics.

As a Spaniard, the whole world wants to know about my holiday experiences in Ibiza, and it comes as a surprise to learn that I have never been to the "party capital of the world." To tell the truth, I would sooner relax on one of the beautiful beaches and stay in an *agroturismo*, a small rural house, and enjoy the countryside and local cuisine. I am getting old! The landscape and local food of all the Balearic Islands are just too good to be missed.

Avocado with shrimp and tomato vinaigrette

When I was a child, it was very rare to find avocados on the Spanish mainland, but you did see them on the islands. Of course, they are now found all over Spain and there are big growers in Andalusia. For this recipe, I marry avocados with shrimp for a classic combination, but please try the tomato vinaigrette with it. The buttery flavor of the avocados, sweetness from the shrimp, and the acidity of the tomatoes make this dish a perfect summer appetizer.

Serves 4

2 ripe, but firm avocados

20 cooked large shrimp, peeled

1 roasted red bell pepper, skinned, seeded, and cut into long thin strips

1 fat scallion, thinly sliced

1 teaspoon chopped flat-leaf parsley

For the tomato vinaigrette

9 oz vine-ripened tomatoes, skinned and seeded

1 small garlic clove, crushed to a paste with a little salt

2 tablespoons red wine vinegar

¼ teaspoon superfine sugar

sea salt and freshly ground black pepper

2–3 tablespoons extra-virgin olive oil, plus extra to serve (depending on the juiciness of the tomatoes)

For the tomato vinaigrette, put the tomato flesh into a mini food processor with the garlic, vinegar, sugar, ½ teaspoon salt, and some pepper, and blend everything together until smooth. With the motor still running, gradually add the olive oil.

Cut each of the avocados in half and remove and discard the pits. Peel off the skin, place cut-side down onto a board and cut the flesh crosswise on the diagonal into thin slices.

Spoon 2 tablespoons of the tomato vinaigrette into the center of 4 small plates. Arrange the avocado slices and peeled shrimps on top. Arrange the red pepper strips in amongst them and then spoon over an additional 2 tablespoons of the dressing. Sprinkle over the onion and chopped parsley, drizzle with a little more oil, and serve with some fresh crusty bread.

Salt-crusted potatoes with cilantro mojo

Everyone thinks that cilantro came from the Americas to Spain because it is eaten there in great quantities, but, believe it or not, the herb was taken there by the *conquistadores*. Cilantro is very popular in the Canary Islands and this *mojo* (sauce) is found everywhere there. This dish of *patatas arrugas* ("wrinkled potatoes") is a perfect tapa for a party, and very healthy because of all the garlic! You can always cut down the amount of garlic if you prefer. Jersey Royals are my favorite potato, but use any type of waxy new potato, such as Fingerling, if they are not available.

Serves 6

2¼ lb evenly sized waxy new potatoes, such as Fingerling, scrubbed but unpeeled

sea salt flakes

For the cilantro mojo

3 large garlic cloves, roughly chopped

1 green chili pepper, seeded and chopped

leaves from a bunch of fresh cilantro, roughly chopped

1 teaspoon freshly ground cumin seeds

scant ½ cup extra-virgin olive oil

2 teaspoons white wine vinegar, Muscatel if possible

Put the potatoes into a wide shallow pan in which they fit in a single layer. Add 2 tablespoons salt and 1 quart cold water (enough just to cover), bring to a boil, and leave to boil rapidly until the water has evaporated. Then turn the heat to low and continue to cook for a few minutes, gently turning the potatoes over occasionally, until they are dry and the skins are wrinkled and covered in a thin crust of salt.

While the potatoes are cooking, make the cilantro *mojo*. Put the garlic, green chili pepper and 1 teaspoon salt in a mortar and pound into a paste. Add the cilantro leaves, and pound until they are incorporated into the paste. Add the cumin, and gradually mix in the oil to make a smooth sauce. Just before serving, stir in the vinegar and spoon into a small bowl.

Pile the hot potatoes onto a plate and serve with the *mojo*, instructing your guests to rub off as much salt from the potatoes as they wish before dipping them into the sauce.

Roasted squash with dried chili pepper, honey, cinnamon, and pine nuts

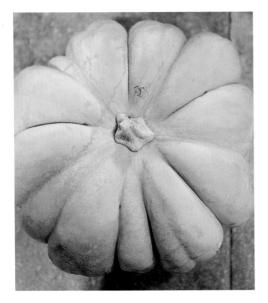

This can be a side dish for any grilled fish or meat. I serve it with Ibérico pork cheeks or any game stew. It is also delicious on its own.

Serves 4–6

3¼ lb unprepared squash (butternut, onion or kabocha)

4 tablespoons olive oil

1 fat garlic clove, finely chopped

½ teaspoon crushed dried red pepper flakes

½ teaspoon ground cinnamon

¼ cup pine nuts

3 tablespoons honey

sea salt flakes and freshly ground black pepper

Preheat the oven to 400°F. Halve the squash through the stem end, scoop out the seeds, peel and then cut into 1–1¼-inch-thick wedges.

Put the oil into a roasting pan with the garlic, red pepper flakes, cinnamon, 1 teaspoon sea salt flakes, and plenty of freshly ground black pepper. Mix well together. Add the wedges of squash to the pan and turn them over a few times in the oil mixture until well coated. Sit them on their curved edges, and roast them in the oven for 20 minutes.

Spread the pine nuts onto a baking sheet and roast them in the oven alongside the squash for 5–6 minutes, giving them a stir occasionally, until they are all golden. Remove and set aside.

Remove the squash from the oven, and brush the wedges with some of the honey. Return to the oven and roast for another 15 minutes, brushing with more of the honey and then the caramelized juices, every 5 minutes, until the squash is tender, and slightly caramelized. Brush one last time with the juices from the pan, pile onto a serving plate, and scatter over the pine nuts.

Scrambled eggs with tomatoes, Serrano ham, and avocado

You might think it's a bit crazy to have scrambled egg with avocado but, with its Latin American influence, this recipe works well, and is delicious served with tortillas.

Serves 4

3 tablespoons olive oil

1 small onion, finely chopped

1 large garlic clove, finely chopped

1 green chili pepper, finely chopped

12 oz vine-ripened tomatoes, skinned, seeded and diced

3 oz Serrano ham, finely chopped

2–3 tablespoons chopped cilantro, plus extra to garnish

8 extra large eggs, beaten

1 small ripe but firm avocado, pitted, peeled and cut into small dice

warm flour tortillas (see page 229), to serve

sea salt and freshly ground black pepper

Heat the olive oil in a medium, deep-sided, nonstick frying pan over medium heat. Add the onion, garlic, chili pepper, and some seasoning, cover and cook gently for 10 minutes until soft. Stir in the tomatoes, cook for 5 minutes, then stir in the ham, and cook for another minute.

Stir in the chopped cilantro, followed by the beaten eggs and diced avocado, and stir over medium-low heat until the eggs are softly scrambled. Spoon onto warmed plates, sprinkle with a little more chopped cilantro, and serve with the warm flour tortillas.

Russian-style corn salad with lobster and homemade chips

I know you will wonder why there is a Russian salad in a Spanish book, but you will find the *ensaladilla Rusa* in restaurants and tapas bars all over Spain, with thousands of variations. It should be called a Spanish summer salad. In the Canaries, they slip in some corn as well. When I told my friend about this dish, he thought I was mad, but I promise it is delicious!

Serves 6–8

2 x 1 lb cooked lobsters

1 large fresh corn on the cob or 1 cup fresh corn kernels

6 oz waxy new potatoes

6 oz carrots, halved

3½ oz fine green beans

⅓ cup petits pois, freshly shelled or frozen

½ quantity Olive Oil Mayonnaise (see page 227)

1½ teaspoons lemon juice

5 scallions, thinly sliced

½ cup gherkins, finely chopped

1 tablespoon chopped flat-leaf parsley

sea salt

For the homemade chips

1¼ lb small, floury potatoes, such as Russet

olive or peanut oil, for deep-frying

First remove the meat from the lobsters. Twist off the claw arms and break each one into 3 pieces at the joints. Crack the shells of each claw with a lobster cracker or large sharp knife, and remove the meat. Slice open the meat from the largest claw, remove the very thin, flat piece of bone from the center, and discard. Remove the meat from the other pieces by hooking them out with a lobster pick. Try to keep the pieces of meat as large as possible. Pull the tail away from the head and discard the head. Place the tail belly-side down on a chopping board and, using a large, sharp knife, cut it in half lengthwise. Separate the two halves and remove and discard the dark intestinal tract that runs along the top edge of the tail meat (there might be a little on each half). Lift out the piece of tail meat from each half, and cut it crosswise into thin slices. Put the meat onto a plate, cover, and chill until you are ready to serve.

For the salad, stand the whole corn cob upright on a board and cut the kernels away, keeping the blade as close to the cob as you can. Cook the vegetables separately in boiling salted water until tender, then refresh them in a bowl of ice water. The potatoes will take about 12–15 minutes, the carrots about 8 minutes, the green beans 4 minutes, the corn 3 minutes, and the peas 1 minute. Drain everything well, cut the potatoes into ½-inch dice, and the carrots and beans into similar-sized pieces.

Mix the mayonnaise with the lemon juice in a mixing bowl, then fold in the cooked vegetables, scallions, chopped gherkins, parsley, and some seasoning to taste.

For the chips, peel the potatoes and slice them crosswise, very thinly, ideally using a mandoline. Wash them in plenty of cold water to remove the starch, and dry well—spin them first in a salad spinner, then dry them extra well on clean kitchen towels. Heat some oil for deep-frying to 350°F. Place a chip basket in the oil, drop in a large handful of the potato slices, and fry for 1½–2 minutes, stirring them around occasionally, until golden brown and very crisp. Remove using the chip basket, shake off the excess oil, then spread the chips over a paper-lined baking sheet and leave to cool. Sprinkle with a little fine sea salt, and set aside.

Spoon some of the salad onto 4 plates, and arrange the lobster meat alongside. Pile some of the chips onto the plate and serve.

Puchero Canario

This is a *cocido*-like stew, served all over the Canaries, but quite different from all others in Spain because it uses vegetables from the New World. It is so popular that you can buy the necessary meat and vegetables pre-packaged in many of the supermarkets. I have simplified the traditional recipe, keeping the key flavors, but making it into more of a chunky stew, which I sometimes serve with a spoonful of spicy red *mojo* (page 212).

Serves 8

3 tablespoons olive oil

10-oz piece of unsmoked ham, cut into
  ½-inch-wide strips

4 x 3½-oz chorizo sausages, skinned, and
  each cut into 6 chunky pieces

1½ lb boneless chicken thigh fillets, cut in half

1 teaspoon crushed dried red pepper flakes

1 large onion, chopped

6 fat garlic cloves, thinly sliced

1 large carrot, cut into small chunks

2 teaspoons freshly ground cumin seeds

1 teaspoon saffron strands, lightly toasted,
  then ground

14 oz cooked chickpeas

1 lb squash, such as kabocha or butternut,
  peeled and cut into small chunky pieces

14 oz sweet potatoes, peeled and cut into
  small chunky pieces

12 oz small waxy new potatoes, such as
  Charlotte, peeled and thickly sliced

2 fresh corn on the cob, cut crosswise into
  ½-inch-thick slices

8 oz fine green beans, cut into 2-inch pieces

7 oz zucchini, cut into ¾-inch dice

12 oz piece of Napa cabbage, cut into
  1-inch-wide strips

sea salt and freshly ground black pepper

Heat the oil in a large flameproof casserole. Add the ham strips and chorizo sausage, and fry for 2 minutes until lightly golden. Remove with a slotted spoon onto a plate and set aside. Season the chicken pieces with salt and pepper, add to the casserole, and fry until lightly golden on both sides. Remove and set aside with the ham and chorizo.

Add the red pepper flakes to the oil left in the pan and, as soon as they start to sizzle, add the onion, garlic, and carrot, cover, and fry gently for 5 minutes until the onion is soft.

Stir in the cumin and saffron, and fry for 2 minutes, then add 1 quart water and bring to a boil. Stir in the chicken, chorizo, ham, and 1 teaspoon salt, cover, and simmer for 15 minutes.

Uncover and stir in the chickpeas, squash, sweet and waxy potatoes, and a little more salt if necessary, re-cover, and simmer for 15 minutes. Uncover, add the corn pieces and green beans, and simmer for 5 minutes, then stir in the zucchini and cabbage, and simmer for another 5 minutes, by which time all the vegetables should be tender. Adjust the seasoning to taste, and serve.

Broiled mackerel with tomato, chili pepper, and mint salad

I often combine oily fish with tomatoes to cut through the richness of the fish, but what can I do? It's the perfect combination. The chili pepper and mint add an extra kick to this beautiful summer salad.

Serves 4

1 garlic clove

1 teaspoon dried oregano

½ teaspoon sweet paprika

2 tablespoons olive oil, plus extra for oiling

4 x 12 oz mackerel, cleaned, gutted, and trimmed of their fins

sea salt and freshly ground black pepper

For the tomato, chili pepper, and mint salad

1¼ lb ripe beef tomatoes, skinned

1 medium-hot red chili pepper, seeded and finely chopped

1 fat scallion, thinly sliced

1 tablespoon red wine vinegar

3 tablespoons extra-virgin olive oil

small bunch of fresh mint leaves

1½ cups small watercress sprigs

Preheat the broiler to high. Crush the clove of garlic on a board under the blade of a large knife, sprinkle with a little salt, and then work it into a paste with the blade. Put the paste into a bowl and mix in the dried oregano, paprika, and oil. Slash the mackerel on the diagonal at ³⁄₈-inch intervals along both sides and brush some of the paprika oil inside the cavity as well as over the skin. Season inside and out, and lay on an oiled baking sheet or the rack of the broiler pan.

For the tomato salad, halve the tomatoes and remove the seeds. Cut the flesh into small chunky pieces, and scatter them over the base of a large serving plate. Sprinkle with some salt and pepper, then the chili pepper and scallion. Whisk the vinegar and oil together with a little more seasoning, and drizzle over the salad, then scatter over the mint, followed by the watercress sprigs. Broil the mackerel for 4–5 minutes on each side until cooked through. Serve with the salad.

Barbecued sardines with mango, red onion, and cilantro salsa

For me, you cannot beat sardines fresh from the sea, cooked on the barbecue and served with some thinly sliced red onion, dressed with a good olive oil and some sherry vinegar to help cut through the oiliness of the fish. The zingy salsa adds another layer of flavor, which results in a really well-balanced dish.

Serves 6

12–16 fresh sardines

For the salsa

1 large ripe but firm mango

1 medium-hot red chili pepper, seeded and finely chopped

½ small red onion, finely chopped

finely grated zest of ½ lime

2 teaspoons lime juice

1 cup cilantro leaves, finely chopped

sea salt and freshly ground black pepper

To prepare the sardines, rub the scales off each fish with your thumb, working under cold running water, then gut them and trim off their fins.

If you are using a charcoal barbecue, light it 30 minutes or so before you want to start cooking. When it is ready to cook on, the coals should be covered in a layer of light gray ash. If using a gas barbecue, light it 10 minutes beforehand.

For the salsa, peel the mango, then slice the flesh away from either side of the flat pit in one piece, and cut into small dice. Mix in a bowl with the remaining ingredients, and set aside.

Barbecue the sardines for 2–3 minutes on each side until the skins blister and char a little, and they are just cooked through. Serve with the salsa.

Pan-fried sardines with tomato and rosemary salsa templada

When I was child, we ate sardines at least once a week—fried, *a la plancha* (grilled on the barbecue), even straight from the basket raw. I love sardines so much. This warm dressing (*templada*) on sardines is my latest addition to the menu at Pizarro, my restaurant.

Serves 4

12 fresh sardines

4 tablespoons olive oil

sea salt and freshly ground black pepper

1 quantity Olive Oil Mashed Potatoes (see page 33), to serve

For the warm tomato dressing

1 small onion, finely chopped

1 garlic clove, finely chopped

1 tablespoon olive oil

9 oz skinned, seeded and chopped tomatoes, fresh or canned

4 tablespoons red wine vinegar

1 teaspoon superfine sugar

3½ oz extra-virgin olive oil

1 tablespoon finely chopped rosemary

To prepare the sardines, rub the scales off each fish with your thumb, working under cold running water, then gut them and trim off the fins. Season them inside and out.

For the tomato dressing, gently fry the onion and garlic in the olive oil until soft, but not browned. Add the tomatoes, and simmer for 10–15 minutes. Meanwhile, put half the red wine vinegar and the sugar into a very small pan, and boil rapidly until reduced to 1 teaspoon. Stir this into the tomato sauce, season well, then blend in a blender until smooth. Return to a clean pan, and simmer if necessary until thick enough to coat the back of a wooden spoon. Keep warm. Put the rest of the vinegar into a bowl with the extra-virgin olive oil, chopped rosemary, and some seasoning and whisk well together. Set aside.

To cook the sardines, heat half the olive oil in a large frying pan, add half the fish and pan-fry for 3 minutes on each side until cooked through, and lightly golden. Lift onto a baking sheet and keep warm while you cook the remainder.

Stir the warm tomato sauce into the herb vinaigrette. Spoon some of the olive oil mashed potato slightly to one side of each of 4 warmed plates, and rest the sardines alongside. Spoon some of the dressing around the edge of the plate and serve.

Sautéed squid, onions, and potatoes with chili pepper and sherry vinegar

This recipe is amazing. I love *calamari a la romana* (deep-fried squid), one of the most popular tapas all over Spain, and synonymous with Spanish cooking, but I think calamari deserves more than that. This is one great example. The most important thing is to caramelize the onions well, so take your time.

Serves 4

⅓ cup extra-virgin olive oil

1 medium onion, halved and thinly sliced

9 oz small waxy potatoes, such as Charlotte, unpeeled

1 lb medium squid, cleaned

½ teaspoon crushed dried red pepper flakes

1 garlic clove, finely chopped

leaves from 2 large fresh thyme sprigs

1 tablespoon sherry vinegar

1 tablespoon chopped flat-leaf parsley

sea salt and freshly ground black pepper

Heat 2 tablespoons of the oil in a large frying pan, add the onion, cover, and cook over medium-low heat, stirring occasionally, for about 15 minutes until it is soft, and nicely caramelized. Meanwhile, cook the potatoes in salted boiling water for 15 minutes until tender. Drain, peel and cut in half lengthwise.

Slice the squid pouches crosswise into ¼-inch-thick rings. Leave the tentacles as they are.

Heat another tablespoon of the oil in a small frying pan and add the potatoes, cut-side down. Fry gently for 2–3 minutes, turning them over half way through, until crisp and nicely golden. Set aside over very low heat.

Heat another tablespoon of the oil in a large frying pan, add half the squid and half the red pepper flakes, season with salt, and fry over high heat for 1½ minutes, adding half the garlic halfway through, until the squid is cooked and nicely caramelized. Transfer to the small frying pan with the potatoes to keep warm, and fry the rest of the squid as before with the remaining oil, red pepper flakes and garlic. Return the first batch of squid, along with the potatoes, to the large pan, sprinkle in the thyme leaves and toss together briefly over medium-high heat to mix them together. Drizzle in the sherry vinegar, add the chopped parsley and caramelized onion, toss together once more, and serve.

Sautéed squid with green beans and toasted almonds

This recipe is all about how to cook your squid perfectly. They must be cooked very quickly, as here, or really slowly—never in between. People don't often put nuts and fish together, but I think the nuttiness of the almonds works well with the squid and adds texture. I developed this recipe with my friend Esperanza and when we tried it, it went straight onto the menu. Even now, in José, I make it with runner beans (pole beans) *a la plancha*, but this dish is definitely the winner (because *a la plancha* means that the juices run out, whereas here you contain the caramelized juices from the squid).

Serves 4

9 oz fine green beans
1 lb medium squid, cleaned
2 tablespoons olive oil
2 garlic cloves, finely chopped
1 medium-hot red chili pepper, seeded and finely chopped
1 tablespoon sherry vinegar
leaves from 2 large fresh thyme sprigs, plus extra to garnish
¼ cup slivered almonds, toasted, plus extra to garnish
sea salt and freshly ground black pepper

Bring a pan of salted water to a boil. Trim the green beans, and cut them in half if very long. Drop them into the boiling water, and cook for 3 minutes. Drain, refresh under cold water, and drain well once more. Set aside.

Slit open the squid pouches along one side, and cut in half lengthwise, then cut each piece crosswise into wide strips. Cut each bunch of tentacles in half. Put half the olive oil and half the garlic into a large frying pan, and as soon as the garlic starts to color, add half the squid, half the chili pepper and some seasoning, and stir-fry over high heat for 2–3 minutes until the squid is just cooked through and lightly caramelized. Transfer to a plate, and repeat with the remaining garlic, squid and chili pepper, but leave everything in the pan.

Return the first batch of squid and the green beans to the pan with the vinegar, and cook briefly over high heat for a few seconds. Add the thyme leaves and toasted slivered almonds and toss well together. Transfer onto a warmed serving plate, scatter with thyme leaves and slivered almonds, and serve.

Lobster with warm lentil salad and romesco sauce

It is quite unusual to see lentils with shellfish; normally lentils are matched with game or meat (see pages 122 and 132). I wanted to try my lobster with romesco sauce and I was looking for more flavor to bring to the dish, and found that the meaty, rich flavor of the lobster went well with the earthy lentils.

Serves 4

4 medium (approx. 1 lb) live lobsters

1 quantity Romesco Sauce (see page 228)

For the warm lentil salad

7 oz pardina lentils (or puy if you can't get hold of pardina lentils)

2 tablespoons olive oil

2 garlic cloves, finely chopped

leaves from 2 large fresh thyme sprigs, plus extra to garnish

1 tablespoon sweet Pedro Ximenez sherry vinegar or balsamic vinegar

sea salt and freshly ground black pepper

Put the live lobsters in the freezer for 1 hour to send them to sleep before cooking.

Check over the lentils for any small stones, then pour into a saucepan and cover by 2 inches with cold water. Bring to a boil, reduce the heat, and leave to simmer for 30 minutes, or until just cooked, adding a little salt to the pan 5 minutes before the end of cooking. Drain well.

Meanwhile, bring one or two large pans of water to a boil, adding 2 tablespoons salt per quart of water. Add the lobsters, bring the water back to a boil and cook for 5 minutes. Remove them from the pan(s) and leave until cool enough to handle. Discard the water.

To remove the meat from the shell, break off the claws, break them open at each joint, and remove the meat from each segment in pieces as large as possible. Break the tails away from the heads, which you can discard. Turn the tail upside down and, holding it in one hand, cut along either side of the flat belly shell with strong scissors. Pull back the flap of shell, and lift out the tail meat. Repeat for each tail.

To finish the lentils, put 1 tablespoon of olive oil and garlic in a medium saucepan and place it over medium heat. As soon as the garlic starts to sizzle, add the thyme leaves and cook gently for 1 minute. Stir in the lentils, and heat through gently. Stir in the vinegar and some seasoning to taste, and keep warm over low heat.

To finish the lobster, heat the remaining olive oil in a large nonstick frying pan over medium heat. Add the lobster tails, and sauté them gently for 2 minutes, turning occasionally, until heated through. Add the claw meat 1 minute before they are ready.

Lift the lobster tails onto a board, and slice each one crosswise into ½-inch-thick slices. Overlap the slices on 4 warmed plates, and arrange the claw meat between the slices. Spoon the lentils next to the lobster, with some of the romesco sauce alongside. Garnish with thyme sprigs and serve.

Lobster caldereta

This is a classic dish from the Balearic Islands where lobster is plentiful. This stew, or *caldereta*, is intensely flavored with garlic and tomatoes, thickened with a paste of garlic, olive oil, parsley, and the tomalley (the lobster liver) at the end. I like to serve the stew on toasted slices of bread spread with a little alioli (garlic mayonnaise), but it is just as good served on toasted bread rubbed with garlic and drizzled with olive oil. Or you can just serve it with some fresh crusty bread for mopping up all the delicious juices.

Serves 4

4 medium (approx. 1 lb) live lobsters

scant ½ cup olive oil

1 medium and 1 small onion, chopped

5 garlic cloves: 1 crushed, 3 sliced, and 1 left whole

1 small carrot, chopped

1 celery stalk, chopped

scant ½ cup brandy

scant ½ cup dry white wine

3 fresh bay leaves

4 large thyme sprigs

1 large red bell pepper, seeded and finely chopped

1¾ lb skinned, seeded and chopped vine-ripened tomatoes, fresh or canned

1 teaspoon superfine sugar

2 tablespoons chopped flat-leaf parsley, plus extra to serve

4 slices of crusty white bread, ½-inch thick

4 heaping teaspoons Alioli (see page 227)

sea salt and freshly ground black pepper

Put the live lobsters in the freezer for 1 hour to send them to sleep before cooking. Bring one or two large pans of water to the boil, adding 2 tablespoons salt per quart of water. Add the lobsters, bring the water back to a boil and cook for 5 minutes. Remove them from the pan(s), and leave until cool enough to handle. Discard the water. Remove the claws and the tails from the lobsters. Cut each tail crosswise into 3 pieces through the shell, break the claws in half at the joint, and crack the shells of each piece to make it easier to remove the meat later on. Break open the heads and use a teaspoon to scoop out the tomalley (the grey-green liver), and any red coral from each piece, and put them in the fridge. Now break the heads and the legs into smaller pieces, and reserve the cracked shells.

Heat 2 tablespoons of the olive oil in a large saucepan. Add the small chopped onion, the crushed garlic clove, the carrot, and the celery, and fry briskly for 5–6 minutes until soft and lightly golden. Add the pieces of lobster shell and fry for 2–3 minutes more. Pour over the brandy, set it alight, and shake the pan until the flames have died down. Add the white wine, and cook until it has almost disappeared, then pour over 5 cups of water, add the bay leaves and thyme stalks (reserve the leaves), and bring to a boil. Cover, and simmer for 30 minutes, then strain through a sieve into a clean pan. Discard the vegetables and shells. Boil the stock rapidly until it has reduced to 2½ cups.

For the stew, heat another 3 tablespoons of the oil in a large casserole over medium heat. Add the large chopped onion, the 3 sliced garlic cloves, and the red bell pepper, cover, and cook for 5 minutes until soft. Add the tomatoes, reserved thyme leaves, sugar, and a little salt, bring to a boil, and simmer uncovered for 20 minutes.

Meanwhile, use a mortar and pestle (or a mini food processor) to pound together the remaining whole garlic clove, the parsley, the remaining oil, the reserved tomalley, and any coral into a smooth paste. Set aside.

Transfer the tomato sauce to a blender and blend until smooth. Return it to the casserole with the stock, season, and bring back to a simmer. Add the lobster pieces and simmer gently for 2 minutes. Stir in the parsley, garlic, and tomalley paste, and simmer for 1 minute. Meanwhile, toast the bread, and spread each slice with a heaping teaspoon of the alioli. Put the toasts into the bottom of 4 large soup plates. Ladle the lobster and sauce into each bowl, and serve sprinkled with parsley.

Chicken, avocado, and melting cheese quesadillas

When you read this recipe, you may think that we're in Mexico, but you will find *quesadillas* **throughout the Islands. I've included it because it's a tasty, fresh, and easy dish to cook for guests when you haven't got much time.**

Serves 4

3 scant tablespoons extra-virgin olive oil
8 x 7-inch soft flour tortillas (see page 229)
1 small cooked chicken, skinned, boned, and shredded
1 large avocado, halved, skinned, pitted, and thinly sliced
4 pickled green chili peppers, drained and thinly sliced
7 oz Mahon cheese (or mature Cheddar), coarsely grated
1 lime, halved
4 heaping tablespoons sour cream
sea salt flakes

For the tomato salsa

7 oz vine-ripened tomatoes, skinned, seeded, and finely chopped
1 green chili pepper, finely chopped
1 large garlic clove, finely chopped
6 scallions, thinly sliced
1 cup fresh cilantro, chopped

Mix the ingredients for the salsa in a bowl, and season to taste with salt. Heat a nonstick frying pan over medium heat. Add 1 teaspoon of the oil, swirl it around, and then place one tortilla in the base of the pan. Spread with one quarter of the tomato salsa, then scatter over a quarter of the chicken, a quarter of the avocado, and 1 pickled chili pepper. Season with a little salt, then sprinkle over a quarter of the grated cheese and a squeeze of lime juice, and dot with 1 heaping tablespoon of the sour cream. Place another tortilla on top and gently press down. This should take you about 2 minutes, by which time the bottom tortilla should be crisp and golden brown. Carefully slide it out onto a plate, add another teaspoon of oil to the pan, and then invert the tortilla sandwich back into the pan, and cook for another 2 minutes. Slide the *quesadilla* onto a board, cut into 6 wedges and serve hot, before cooking the next one in the same way.

Tortilla soup with choricero peppers, roasted green chili peppers, and lime

This is an excellent soup with overtones from the New World, incorporating local ingredients, which is ideal for using up any leftover stale corn tortillas. It is spicy and fresh at the same time, and a comfort food. You can always change the ingredients to make use of any leftovers you have.

Serves 4

1½ oz dried choricero peppers (or other mild, smoky chili peppers, such as ancho or pasilla)

6–7 tablespoons extra-virgin olive oil

2 fat garlic cloves, halved

2 medium-hot green chili peppers, halved and seeded

7 oz skinned, chopped vine-ripened tomatoes, fresh or canned

1 medium onion, halved and thinly sliced

1 teaspoon crushed dried red pepper flakes

1½ quarts homemade chicken stock

6 x day-old corn tortillas (see page 229)

7 oz cooked chicken, skinned and shredded

8 oz young Swiss chard, shredded, or baby spinach leaves

juice of 1 large lime (approx. 2 tablespoons)

2 cups fresh cilantro, roughly chopped

4 oz Spanish cheese, such as Manchego or Idiazabel, coarsely grated, to serve

sea salt flakes

Slit open the choricero peppers and remove and discard the stalks and seeds. Tear each one into 4 wide flat strips. Heat a dry frying pan over medium heat, add the strips of dried pepper, skin-side down, and toast them for a few seconds until they darken slightly. Transfer them to a bowl, cover with boiling water, and leave them to soak for 30 minutes.

Meanwhile, add 1 teaspoon of the oil to the frying pan, add the halved garlic cloves and fry gently until golden brown. Remove to a plate, add the green chili peppers, and fry gently for 3–4 minutes until soft and lightly colored. Set aside with the garlic. Drain the soaked peppers, and scrape the flesh away from the skins. Discard the skins. Put the fried garlic cloves, green chili peppers, tomatoes, and choricero pepper flesh into a mini food processor, and blend to a smooth paste.

Heat 2 tablespoons of the oil in a medium saucepan. Add the onion and red pepper flakes, cover, and fry gently for 6–8 minutes until the onion is soft and lightly golden. Add the garlic and tomato paste to the fried onion, and fry for 5 minutes until the mixture thickens. Add the chicken stock, bring to a boil, and leave to simmer, uncovered, for 30 minutes.

Meanwhile, cut the corn tortillas into 2-inch-wide strips. Heat the remaining oil in a frying pan, add one-third of the tortilla strips and fry until crisp and lightly golden. Set aside to drain on paper towels while you cook the remainder.

To finish the dish, stir the chicken and Swiss chard or spinach into the soup, and simmer for 2 minutes. Stir in the lime juice, cilantro, and some salt to taste. Ladle into bowls, sprinkle with the fried tortilla strips and grated cheese, and serve.

Spiced chicken and tomato sauté

This is a simple everyday supper dish, spiced up with flavors from the Americas, which I like to serve with steamed rice. I never used that many spices until I came to London and started working with David Eyre, and it has inspired me to adapt so many classical Spanish dishes to give them my own twist.

Serves 4

4 tablespoons olive oil

1 x 3¼ lb chicken, cut into 8 pieces

1 medium onion, finely chopped

4 garlic cloves, crushed

2 jalapeño (medium–hot green) peppers, seeded and finely chopped

1 teaspoon sweet paprika

1½ teaspoons ground cumin

3¼ inch cinnamon stick

8 cloves

1 tablespoon chopped oregano

1 lb skinned, chopped tomatoes, fresh or canned

2 tablespoons tomato paste

$2/3$ cup chicken stock

2 tablespoons lemon juice

$3/8$ cup raisins

½ cup pitted green olives, finely chopped

3 tablespoons chopped fresh cilantro

sea salt and freshly ground black pepper

1 hard-boiled egg, coarsely chopped, to garnish

steamed rice, to serve

Heat the oil in a large deep sauté pan. Season the chicken pieces well with salt and pepper, and fry over medium heat until richly golden all over. Lift the pieces of chicken onto a plate, and pour off all but 2 tablespoons of the fat.

Add the onion, garlic and jalapeño peppers to the pan, and fry for 5 minutes until soft. Add the paprika, cumin, cinnamon stick, cloves, and oregano, and cook for another minute. Stir in the tomatoes, tomato paste, chicken stock, lemon juice, raisins, and half the olives, and leave to simmer for 5 minutes.

Return the chicken pieces to the pan, spoon over some of the sauce, cover, and simmer for 15–20 minutes, until the chicken is cooked through, and the sauce has reduced and slightly thickened.

Stir in the chopped cilantro, and adjust the seasoning to taste. Scatter over the rest of the olives and the hard-boiled egg, and serve with steamed rice.

Chargrilled rabbit with spicy red and avocado green mojos

You must do this recipe once in your life. Try to buy wild rabbit if you can because the sauces can cope with the flavor, but feel free to use these sauces for chicken, lamb, or any barbecued meat. Once again, you can see the Latin American influences in the *mojos*. Your guests will love them.

Serves 4

2 x 3¼ lb wild or farmed rabbits

3 garlic cloves

6 tablespoons extra-virgin olive oil

juice of 1 lemon (approx. 3 tablespoons)

1 teaspoon dried oregano

leaves from 2 x 5-inch rosemary sprigs, finely chopped

2 teaspoons fennel seeds, crushed

sea salt flakes and freshly ground black pepper

patatas fritas, to serve (see page 117)

For the spicy red mojo

3 dried red choricero peppers

1½ tablespoons sherry vinegar

4½ tablespoons extra-virgin olive oil

pinch of superfine sugar

3 garlic cloves

¾ teaspoon sweet paprika

¾ teaspoon crushed dried red pepper flakes

1 teaspoon freshly ground cumin seeds

For the avocado green mojo

3 tablespoons sherry vinegar

scant ⅔ cup extra-virgin olive oil

pinch of superfine sugar

6 garlic cloves

½ teaspoon crushed dried red pepper flakes

1 ripe avocado, skinned, pitted and roughly chopped

½ teaspoon freshly ground cumin seeds

2 cups cilantro leaves

Cut up the rabbits according to the instructions on page 215, but cut each saddle into 3 pieces and leave the hind legs whole.

Crush the garlic cloves on a board under the blade of a large knife, sprinkle with a little salt, then work into a paste with the blade. Put the paste into a large shallow baking dish and mix in the oil, lemon juice, oregano, rosemary, fennel seeds, and plenty of freshly ground black pepper. Add the rabbit pieces and mix well together. Cover, refrigerate, and leave to marinate for 4–12 hours, turning the pieces occasionally.

If you are using a charcoal barbecue, light it 30 minutes or so before you want to start cooking. When it is ready to cook on, the coals should be covered in a layer of light gray ash. If using a gas barbecue, light it 10 minutes beforehand.

Shortly before you are ready to cook the rabbit, make the *mojos*. For the spicy red *mojo*, slit open the choricero peppers and discard the stalks and seeds. Cover with boiling water and leave to soak for 30 minutes. Then drain, scrape the flesh away from the skins, and discard the skins. Whisk the sherry vinegar with the olive oil, sugar, and ½ teaspoon sea salt flakes. Put the red pepper flesh, garlic, paprika, red pepper flakes, cumin seeds, and another ½ teaspoon sea salt into a mini food processor, and blend to a smooth paste. Then, with the motor still running, gradually add the sherry vinaigrette to make a smooth sauce.

For the avocado green *mojo*, whisk the sherry vinegar with the olive oil, sugar, and ½ teaspoon sea salt flakes. Put the garlic, red pepper flakes, avocado, cumin, cilantro leaves, and another ½ teaspoon sea salt flakes into a mini food processor, and blend to a smooth paste. Then, with the motor still running, gradually add the sherry vinaigrette to make a smooth sauce. Season to taste with a little more salt if necessary.

Lift the rabbit pieces out of the marinade and shake off the excess. Place them onto the barbecue, and cook for 6 minutes on each side for the smaller pieces, 7–8 minutes for the larger pieces of saddle and the hind legs, brushing them with some of the leftover marinade occasionally, until they are golden brown and cooked through. Pile the pieces onto a warmed serving plate, and serve with the spicy red and avocado green *mojos* and some *patatas fritas* (fried potatoes).

Rabbit salmorejo

This is a signature dish of the Canary Islands; in many ways not that dissimilar to an *escabeche*, and bears no relation to the thick tomato soup from Cordoba with the same name. Make sure you marinate your rabbit for at least 6 hours, but preferably 12 hours, so that the flavors have time to get right into the meat before you cook it. This is often served with *patatas fritas*, which I love, but because the sauce is quite liquid, I think it also goes extremely well with steamed rice.

Serves 4

3¼ lb farmed rabbit

6 garlic cloves, crushed

1 tablespoon sweet paprika

1 medium-hot red chili pepper, seeded and finely chopped

6 tablespoons extra-virgin olive oil

3 tablespoons red wine vinegar or sherry vinegar

scant 1 cup dry white wine

leaves from a 4-inch rosemary sprig, finely chopped

leaves from 1 large thyme sprig

2 medium onions, cut into thin wedges

3 fresh bay leaves

⅔ cup chicken stock

small bunch of flat-leaf parsley sprigs, roughly chopped

small bunch cilantro sprigs, roughly chopped

sea salt and freshly ground black pepper

patatas fritas (see page 117), roast potatoes, or steamed rice, to serve

To cut up the rabbits, cut off the heads and discard. Cut off the front legs, and remove and discard the bony ends. Cut off the hind legs, and chop them in half through the bone with a cleaver. Then trim away the belly flap from the body section with scissors and cut each saddle crosswise into 4 pieces, leaving the kidneys in place. Put the pieces in a large, shallow baking dish.

Crush the garlic into a paste with ½ teaspoon salt using a mortar and pestle. Add the paprika and red chili pepper, and continue to crush into a paste, then stir in 3 tablespoons of the olive oil, the vinegar, and 1 teaspoon freshly ground black pepper. Pour the mixture over the rabbit with the wine, rosemary, and thyme, and mix well together. Cover and refrigerate for up to 24 hours, turning the pieces occasionally.

The next day, lift the rabbit pieces out of the marinade, shake off as much of it as you can, and then season them with a little more salt. Keep the marinade. Heat 2 tablespoons of the remaining oil in a large flameproof casserole, and fry the rabbit pieces in batches until nicely browned all over. Lift onto a plate and set aside.

Add the remaining olive oil and the onions to the pan, and fry them until they are soft and lightly golden. Return the rabbit pieces to the casserole and pour over the marinade, stock, and bay leaves. Bring to a simmer, cover, and cook for 40 minutes, or until the rabbit is tender.

Lift the bay leaves from the pan and discard. If you like a smoother sauce, lift the pieces of rabbit onto a plate, pour everything else left in the pan into a food processor, and whizz until smooth. Return the mixture to the pan with the rabbit, and reheat for 5 minutes. Transfer the rabbit onto a serving plate, spoon over the sauce, garnish with the parsley and cilantro, and serve with fried potatoes, roast potatoes, or steamed rice.

Roulade with banana, rum, and brown sugar cream

Branzo de gitano is the cake I always had for my birthday when I was young. It's a roulade covered with cream, and stuffed with custard. It's lovely, but this recipe, that I made with leftover bananas, is just so good. The first time I made it, I ate the whole thing! It's a good way to use over-ripe bananas.

Serves 8

melted butter, for greasing

1 scant cup all-purpose flour, plus extra
  for dusting

4 extra large eggs

½ cup superfine sugar, plus 3 tablespoons

2¼ tablespoons light soft brown sugar

2 tablespoons warm water

2 teaspoons vanilla extract

For the banana cream

3 small, ripe bananas (those marked with
  dark brown spots)

2 tablespoons light soft brown sugar

2 tablespoons dark rum

scant 1 cup heavy cream

Preheat the oven to 375°F. Line a 10 x 15-inch jelly roll pan with parchment paper, brush it with melted butter and then dust it with flour and knock out the excess.

Whisk the eggs, ½ cup of the superfine sugar, and the light soft brown sugar together in a large mixing bowl until the mixture is very thick and mousse-like, and leaves a trail behind on the surface when drizzled from the beaters. Whisk in the warm water and the vanilla extract. Sift over and gently fold in the flour, one third at a time.

Pour the mixture into the prepared pan and tilt it backwards and forwards so that it fills the corners, and forms a thin, even layer. Bake for 12–15 minutes until the center of the cake feels slightly spongy, and the sides have shrunk away slightly from the sides of the pan.

Place a large sheet of parchment paper onto the work surface and sprinkle it with the remaining superfine sugar. Turn out the cake onto this, and remove the lining paper. Place a slightly damp tea towel over the cake, and leave it to cool for 30 minutes.

For the banana cream, peel the bananas, slice them into a bowl, and crush them into a paste using the back of a fork. Mix the brown sugar and rum together until the sugar has dissolved. Whip the cream, and as it begins to thicken, add the rum mixture and continue beating until the cream forms soft peaks. Fold in the mashed bananas.

Using a sharp knife, trim away the crisp edges from each long side of the cake, then score a line 1 inch in from one long edge. Spread over the banana cream. Then, starting with the scored edge nearest to you, firmly roll up the cake.

To serve, cut the roulade into 4 even-sized pieces, then cut each piece on the diagonal into triangles. Place the straight-cut side down onto each plate (so that the top cut face is the sloping one), and serve.

Pan-fried bananas with brandy and orange butter

Please use medium-ripe bananas for this recipe. This is one of the first dishes I cooked when I was studying, but the orange butter is my adaptation of the original dish.

Serves 4

1¼ cups freshly squeezed orange juice
   (from approx. 4 oranges)

4 large ripe but firm bananas

3 tablespoons butter

3 tablespoons light brown sugar

1 tablespoon brandy

1 tablespoon water

large pinch of salt

chilled coconut cream, to serve

Put the orange juice into a small pan and simmer vigorously until reduced to about 3 tablespoons.

Peel the bananas and cut in half crosswise, then cut each piece in half lengthwise. Heat a large nonstick frying pan over medium-high heat. Add 2 tablespoons of the butter, and leave until it has melted and turned nutty-brown. Add the banana pieces and sauté them for 1 minute, turning over halfway through, until lightly browned and just tender. Add 1 tablespoon of the sugar, and shake the pan gently until the sugar has dissolved, then lift the bananas into 4 warmed shallow serving bowls.

Add the remaining sugar, the reduced orange juice, brandy, water, remaining butter, and salt to the pan and simmer for 1 minute. Drizzle the sauce over the bananas and serve with the chilled coconut cream.

Pineapple, chili pepper, lime, and mint served with pineapple and lime sorbet

This chili pepper and lime syrup has quite a kick to it, which I love, but do use just half a chili pepper if you prefer. One pineapple makes quite a lot of sorbet, but it keeps in the freezer for up to 3 months, and is great to have as a standby. I love to add some cava to the sorbet for a nice refreshing drink after a long lunch in the sun...

Serves 6–8

1 large, really ripe and juicy pineapple

10 fresh mint leaves, finely shredded, to serve

For the pineapple and lime sorbet

1 heaping cup superfine sugar

1 cup water

6 juicy limes

1 tablespoon liquid glucose

1 large, really ripe and juicy pineapple

For the chili pepper and lime syrup

¼ cup superfine sugar

finely grated zest and juice of 1 lime

½–1 small medium-hot red chili pepper, seeded and very finely chopped

For the sorbet, put the sugar and water into a pan, and leave over low heat until the sugar has dissolved. Then increase the heat slightly, and simmer for 5 minutes. Meanwhile, finely zest and juice the limes. Remove the syrup from the heat, and stir in the glucose syrup and lime zest. Leave to cool to room temperature, then stir in the lime juice.

Slice the top and bottom off the pineapple, sit it upright on a board, and slice away the skin and all the little brown "eyes." Cut the fruit lengthwise in half, and remove the core with an apple corer. Roughly chop the flesh, put it into a food processor, and blend until smooth. Strain in the lime-flavored syrup, and blend once more until smooth. Pour the mixture into a bowl, cover and chill overnight.

The next day, churn the sorbet mixture in an ice cream maker. Alternatively, pour the mixture into a shallow plastic container, cover and freeze until firm, but not rock hard. Scoop into a food processor and blend until smooth. Return to the container and freeze once again. Repeat the process 2–3 times more, then leave in the freezer until needed.

For the chili pepper and lime syrup, put the sugar and 3 tablespoons water into a small pan and leave to dissolve over low heat. Bring to a boil and boil for 3 minutes, then remove from the heat and stir in the strained lime juice and chopped red chili pepper. Allow to become cold, then stir in the lime zest.

Prepare the second pineapple as before, then lay each piece cut-side down on a board and cut crosswise into very thin slices. Slightly overlap these over the base of 6–8 dessert plates. Cover and chill until needed.

Just before serving, remove the sorbet from the freezer, and allow it to soften slightly at room temperature for 15–20 minutes. Drizzle the chili pepper and lime syrup over the pineapple, and sprinkle with the shredded mint. Top with a scoop of the pineapple and lime sorbet, and serve.

Caramelized pineapple in black pepper and star anise syrup

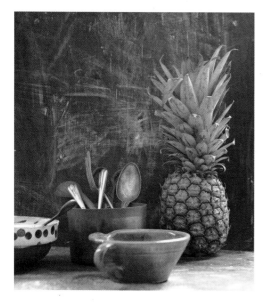

This is quite an unusual recipe, but I love it because the caramelized pineapple is like candy. It's a great dinner party dish.

Serves 4

1 large ripe pineapple

1¼ cups superfine sugar

1 quart water

2 whole star anise

1 teaspoon freshly ground black pepper

Pineapple and Lime sorbet (see page 220) or vanilla ice cream, to serve

Slice the top and bottom off the pineapple, sit it upright on a board and slice away the skin and all the little brown "eyes." Then cut the fruit lengthwise into quarters, slice away the hard core, and cut each piece in half lengthwise again, and then cut each piece crosswise in half.

Put ¾ cup of the sugar and the water into a medium saucepan, and slowly bring to a boil, stirring the sugar to dissolve it. Add the pineapple pieces, bring back to a simmer and cook gently for 15–20 minutes, depending on the ripeness of your pineapple, until tender, but not too soft.

When the pineapple is cooked, carefully lift the pieces into a bowl. Return the syrup to the heat, and boil rapidly until reduced to about 2 cups. Allow to cool, then pour through a sieve back over the pineapple, cover, and chill overnight.

The next day lift the pineapple out of the syrup onto a baking sheet. Pour the syrup into a pan, and boil rapidly until reduced to 1 cup. Add the star anise, and simmer for 1 minute more. Remove from the heat, stir in the black pepper, and leave to go cold.

To serve, pour any excess syrup away from the tray and then sprinkle the pineapple heavily with half the remaining sugar. Caramelize, ideally with a blowtorch, or under a very hot broiler, until golden and bubbling. Turn the pieces over and repeat. Lift the pineapple onto dessert plates and spoon over a little coarsely ground black pepper and star anise syrup. Serve with pineapple and lime sorbet, or vanilla ice cream.

Sticky date and preserved ginger puddings with toffee sauce

I know you must be thinking this sounds like a very English, classic sticky toffee pudding, but I use the dates from the Islands, and I just love this recipe. The longer I live in London, the more British cooking is having an influence on me!

Serves 8

½ stick butter, melted, plus extra for greasing

1¼ cups dates, chopped

4 balls preserved ginger in syrup, finely chopped

1 heaping teaspoon baking soda

1 teaspoon vanilla extract

1 cup boiling water

heaping ¾ cup light brown sugar

2 large eggs, beaten

1⅓ cups self-rising flour

light cream, to serve

For the toffee sauce

1¼ cups heavy cream

¾ stick butter

heaping ¾ cup light brown sugar

Preheat the oven to 350°F. Lightly butter 8 individual 7-oz nonstick pudding molds and base-line with disks of parchment paper.

Mix the dates, preserved ginger, baking soda and vanilla extract in a bowl. Stir in the boiling water, and leave to soften for 5 minutes. Pour the mixture into a food processor, add the butter and sugar, and process briefly until the ingredients are finely chopped, but not a purée. Pour the mixture into a bowl, and stir in the eggs and flour.

Divide the mixture between the prepared molds and bake for 20 minutes or until a toothpick pushed into the center of the puddings comes away clean.

Meanwhile, for the sauce, put the cream, butter, and sugar into a small saucepan and leave over low heat, stirring occasionally until smooth.

When the puddings are cooked, run a knife around the rim of each one and turn them out onto warmed serving plates. Remove the disks of parchment paper, and pour some of the toffee sauce over each pudding. Serve with extra sauce and light cream.

Almond and honey creams with lemon verbena peaches

This is my interpretation of the first time I tried almond and honey creams in a restaurant in Lanzarote and thanks to my memory, I can't remember the name! They were using bananas from the islands, caramelized, but I decided to use peaches instead as they go so well with the flavor of the almonds and give a refreshing and sophisticated feel to the dish.

Serves 6

2 teaspoons powdered gelatin

1¼ cups heavy cream

scant ½ cup whole milk

6 tablespoons honey

7 fl oz carton almond cream (or extra heavy cream)

1–2 drops pure almond extract (optional)

For the lemon verbena peaches

2 large, ripe and juicy peaches

2 teaspoons superfine sugar

2 teaspoons finely chopped lemon verbena or lemon thyme leaves

2 teaspoons lemon juice

Put 2 tablespoons water into a very small saucepan, sprinkle over the gelatin and leave to soak for 5 minutes. Meanwhile, warm the heavy cream, milk, and honey together in another small pan. Dissolve the gelatin over low heat until clear, then stir into the cream with the almond cream (or extra heavy cream) and almond extract (if using).

Pour the mixture into 6 x 5 fl oz glass dessert tumblers. Cover with plastic wrap and chill for at least 6 hours, or until set.

Shortly before serving, peel the peaches (see page 176), halve them, remove the pits and cut the flesh into thin slices. Put them into a bowl with the sugar, lemon verbena, or lemon thyme and lemon juice, and mix together gently. Leave at room temperature for 15–20 minutes.

Remove the almond creams from the fridge, spoon some of the peaches into each glass and serve.

BASIC RECIPES

Olive oil mayonnaise

Makes approx. 1¼ cups

2 large free-range (cage-free) egg yolks,
    at room temperature

2 teaspoons lemon juice

1 teaspoon Dijon mustard

½ teaspoon sea salt flakes

⅔ cup extra-virgin olive oil

⅔ cup sunflower oil

Put the egg yolks, lemon juice, mustard, and sea salt into a mixing bowl, and lightly blend together. Gradually whisk in the oils, a little at a time, until you have produced a thick and silky-smooth mayonnaise.

Alioli

Makes approx. ¾ cup

2 large free-range (cage-free) egg yolks,
    at room temperature

1 small garlic clove, finely chopped,
    or crushed to a paste with the salt

1 teaspoon lemon juice

¼ teaspoon fine sea salt

⅔ cup extra-virgin olive oil

Put the egg yolks into a mixing bowl with the garlic, lemon juice, and salt. Whisk them together, then very gradually whisk in the olive oil, until you have a glistening sauce with the consistency of soft butter. Cover and chill until needed.

BASIC RECIPES

Romesco sauce

Makes approx. 1 cup

2 dried ñora peppers

9 oz vine-ripened tomatoes

2 tablespoons extra-virgin olive oil

3 tablespoons blanched almonds

3 tablespoons hazelnuts, skinned

1 x ½-oz slice of crustless white bread

1 fat garlic clove

1½ teaspoons sherry vinegar

sea salt flakes and freshly ground
   black pepper

Slit open the dried peppers and discard the stalks and seeds. Cover with boiling water and leave to soak for 2 hours.

Preheat the broiler to high. Halve the tomatoes and place them skin-side up on a lightly oiled baking sheet. Broil for about 5 minutes until the skins are black, and the flesh is cooked. Remove the skins, drop the tomatoes into a food processor and leave to cool.

Put the olive oil into a frying pan over medium heat, add the almonds and hazelnuts, and fry until golden brown. Remove with a slotted spoon to a plate and leave to cool. Add the slice of bread and the garlic to the pan, and again fry until they are golden brown. Set aside with the nuts and leave to cool. Remove the pan from the heat.

Scrape the flesh from the soaked peppers with a spoon, and discard the skins. Add the flesh to the food processor with the fried nuts, bread, garlic, sherry vinegar, and any leftover oil from the frying pan. Blend, using the pulse button, into a coarse paste, then season to taste. This can be used immediately, or will keep in the fridge for several days.

Flour tortillas

2²/₃ cups all-purpose flour, plus extra
for dusting

2 teaspoons baking powder

1 teaspoon salt

scant ½ cup chilled lard, cut into small pieces

7 fl oz lukewarm water

Sift the flour, baking powder, and salt into the bowl of a food processor, add the lard, and whizz together briefly until the mixture looks like fine bread crumbs. Pour the mixture into a bowl, stir in the warm water, and mix together into a soft dough. Turn out onto a lightly floured surface, and knead briefly until smooth. If making large tortillas, say for *quesadillas* (see page 208), cut the dough into 8 even-sized pieces. If you want smaller tortillas, cut the dough into 12 pieces. Roll each one into a ball between the palms of your hands. Put onto a plate, cover with a layer of plastic wrap and leave to rest for 1 hour.

To cook the tortillas, heat a dry, heavy-based frying pan over medium heat. Take one ball of dough and flatten it slightly in a little flour, first on one side, and then the other, into a disk. Roll out thinly, giving it a slight turn now and then, into either a 7-inch disc or a 4–5-inch disc. Place the tortilla into the hot pan, and cook for about 15–20 seconds until it is marked with dark spots, then turn over and cook for another 20 seconds. Flip it back over, and cook for 10 seconds more, then flip one last time and cook for another 10 seconds. Remove, and wrap in a clean kitchen towel to keep warm while you cook the remainder in the same way.

Corn tortillas

These make a great wheat-free, gluten-free alternative to bread.

Makes 12

1¼ cups *masa harina* (Mexican corn flour)

6–7 fl oz hot water

salt

Sift the *masa harina* and 1 teaspoon salt into a mixing bowl, and gradually stir in enough hot water to make a slightly moist dough. Cover, and set aside for 15 minutes. Then divide the dough into 12 even-sized pieces, and roll them into balls. Working with one ball at a time, roll or press it out between 2 small squares of parchment paper or plastic wrap into a 5-inch disk.

To cook the tortillas, heat a dry, heavy-based frying pan over medium heat. Peel the paper or plastic wrap from one tortilla, add it to the pan, and cook for about 45 seconds, until lightly colored with little brown spots. Flip it over and cook for another 45 seconds, by which time it should be puffing up and lightly browned on the underside. Wrap each tortilla in a clean kitchen towel as you cook it to keep it warm, and stop it drying out. Cook the remainder in the same way.

SPANISH FLAVORS: INDEX

ACKNOWLEDGMENTS

I want to say a huge thank you to my Mom and Dad—this book is dedicated to you.

And a big thank you to Debbie Major for helping me with the book. I had a lovely time testing and writing the recipes with you.

To my sister Isabel and my brother Antonio and sister-in-law Maria Jose; my nieces and nephews Carmen, Juan, Marina, Antonio and Cristina, for their great support and inspiration.

To Peter for his patience and help in tasting new recipes.

To Sophie Allen for your patience and help, to Kyle Cathie and all the team at Kyle Books.

To Emma Lee, for her friendship and for doing a wonderful job taking beautiful photographs for the book.

Gracias to Hannah Norris for her never-ending hard work.

To my agent Martine Carter for your help.

To Rick Stein for your support and all the team at Denhams TV, especially Arezoo for a great time filming in Spain.

To my business partners Herve, Gavin, Michael and Nialll for your confidence in my projects.

To Catriona for all her help with my website.

To all the staff and friends at *José* and *Pizarro*—too many to say names!

To all my neighbors and friends in Bermondsey Street for making me feel at home.

And to all the British and Spanish press for their support!